A COMPASS FOR THE JOURNEY

By
Betty Dilday

*Betty Dilday
Christmas 2008*

DEDICATION

To Russell, my husband,
with whom we have endeavored together
to follow this compass for fifty-five years.

TABLE OF CONTENTS

INTRODUCTION: WHAT IS YOUR COMPASS?

"Trust in the Lord with all your heart, and lean not on your own understanding. In all your ways acknowledge Him and he will make your paths straight."
(Proverbs 3:5-6)

As a girl, I didn't know much about a compass. I knew they came in all sizes, were round with a black needle inside, had glass on them, and were supposed to give direction to north, south, east, and west.

Webster's dictionary has twelve definitions for compass. (That's one of the reasons why the English language is so difficult.) But the one that I'm interested in is "a compass is an instrument for showing direction, especially one consisting of a magnetic needle swinging freely on a pivot and pointing to the magnetic north."

When I married R.H. Dilday, a former Eagle Scout, I learned a lot more about compasses! Not many years after we were married, Russell learned to fly private planes. He took lessons from a church member, Dave Wilson, who was a Delta pilot and a flight instructor. As our children grew, we not only did a lot of flying, but also in the 80's we bought a sailboat and learned to sail on Eagle Mountain Lake in Ft. Worth. Our friend, Bill Sullivan, who came to Ft. Worth from the east coast of Rhode Island, said *real* sailing had to be on the Atlantic! However, we enjoyed our brown teak wood Boston Whaler, and later a 22 foot blue and white Catalina on the beautiful lake.

In a plane or a sailboat, it's necessary to have a compass to show direction, but it is even more important in your life journey. We've heard the story of the pilot who announced to the passengers on the intercom, "Ladies and gentlemen, I have some bad news and some good news. The bad news is, we've lost power on our compass and we're lost. But the good news is, we have a tail wind and we're really making good time."

Tragically, this is the experience of many people today. They have lost their direction, but they're excited that they're making good time. Time is all too short for one to be going in the wrong direction in the journey of life.

When I was nine years old in the First Baptist Church of Houston, Texas, I publicly accepted Jesus Christ as my Savior and Lord. In trusting Him through these many years, I've realized that He not only promises me life after death, but He is giving me a happier and better life than I could have ever chosen.

There have been unexpected turns along the way but as Catherine Marshall has testified, "He was there helping me on every curve." In all the straight ways and in all the turns of my life Jesus Christ has been my compass. What is your compass?

A COMPASS FOR GUIDANCE

WHEN THE AIR BECOMES TURBULENT, TIGHTEN YOUR SEATBELT

"Cast your cares on the Lord, and He
will sustain you."
(Psalm 55:22)

For many years my husband flew a small single-engine airplane. We had some good family trips, flying to special meetings in Texas and later in the southeast. Russell was a very careful pilot and we never had any "close calls" or any particular moments of fear. Any time the weather ahead became uncertain, we would always "do a 180°" and fly back to our departure airport, rent a car and continue our journey on land. Of course, later we had to go back for the plane!

One very hot summer day we were flying from Atlanta to Dallas. Just as we were approaching Greenville, Texas the air became so bumpy, I couldn't stay in my seat. I was thrown upward toward the ceiling, almost bumping my head. To say the least, I was alarmed, "What's happening?" Russell explained that when the hot, steamy, summer air rises in the afternoons, it produces turbulence. While extreme turbulence can be dangerous, the kind we were experiencing was no problem, just uncomfortable. We both laughed as I continued to rise and fall in my seat. Needless to say, I tightened my seatbelt, and we soon passed through the rough air to smooth flying.

We live in a world of disorderly, agitating, and upsetting situations. Just when we are sailing smoothly through life, these unexpected interruptions suddenly toss us around like turbulence in an airplane cockpit. It may be an unexpected death, some heart-breaking sorrow, a family crisis, a friend's illness, accidents, or a financial loss. These bumpy encounters may be short lived, but they are frightening and threaten our peace of mind and outlook on life.

God knows our vulnerability, and when crises come to our lives, He doesn't want us to be defeated victims but victorious victors. In Romans 8:35 we read *"Who shall separate us from the love of Christ? Shall trouble or hardship or persecution or famine, or nakedness or danger or sword?...No, in all of these things we are more than conquerors through Him who loved us."*

I remember two young couples who encountered terrible turbulence that could have easily defeated them. However, their faith saw them through, and they became examples to everyone who knew them. Lori and Bruce had completed their seminary studies and were on their way to pastor their first church. Bruce had gone on with their furnishings in a u-haul truck and Lori and her mother with their four months old baby were following in a packed car with their remaining possessions. Halfway to their destination, a heavy 18 wheeler truck in front of them lost a hot piece of smoking rubber from a blown out tire.

When Lori's car drove over it, the burning rubber got stuck underneath the car and sparked a fire. Seeing smoke coming from beneath the car, Lori pulled over to the side of the road. Her mother opened the door of the passenger side to look under the car. Flames suddenly flared up and burned her mother badly. As Lori stepped out on her side, flames engulfed the whole front of the car. Reaching frantically into the back seat for her baby, Lori was also burned. Their car and possessions were lost but two frightened women, hurt but safe, could only say how grateful they were that "the turbulence" had not been worse.

Kathy and Don had been married eight years. Many of their friends were pregnant and she wanted to be also. How excited she was when she learned she was going to have a baby. The day before the delivery date she didn't feel any movement from the baby, and she called her doctor. Rushing to the hospital her perfect baby was born without life. Later, out of her deep sorrow, she showed me how trusting in God's love for her saw her through the turbulent tragedy.

How can we cope with turbulence in our lives?

(1) Before we begin to feel sorry for ourselves, we need to quickly think of the blessings that we've already received from God. No matter how large or small the blessing, we should name them and give thanks to God. When Dan Vestal preached a revival at Southwestern seminary, he asked the students in the congregation to call out something for which they were thankful. We heard "good health," "our professors," "God's calling in our lives," and then as silence hung in the air a moment, someone called out, "the $93.60 check that came in today's mail!" The first step in overcoming a crisis is to be truly grateful for what God has already done.

(2) In order to be conquerors we must accept and utilize change. Change is everywhere – like the air we breathe, and our reaction to change can make us fearful or hopeful, sad or joyful. To really live with a strong faith, we must know how to accept change and use it.

(3) Hold to a positive attitude. When we live with the confident hope that God is good, His promises are true, and that He wants us to experience the best in life, then we discover the courage we need to face whatever life may bring. We can say with Job, *"Though He slay me, yet will I hope in Him."*

Robert Louis Stevenson, the renowned writer of novels and poetry, spent a lifetime in poor health, but he always maintained a happy spirit. When he was asked how he could be happy so much of the time, he responded, "I'm, not going to let my life be regulated by a row of medicine bottles."

(4) Maintain a daily relationship with Christ through His word. Gail McDonald calls this action "tending the fire." Remember the time that you accepted Christ and stand firm on the commitment that you made to follow Him. Life's pressures can only be carried if you are in touch with Christ daily. Conquerors over crises are those who make Christ and His will the priority of their lives.

Matthew 5:8 says *"blessed are the pure in heart..."* Happy are those who have a heart that wants to see things from God's perspective and do His will. That's what Corrie Ten Boom meant when she said, "When God is second, you will come out second best, but when God is really first, you will always come out first."

According to Richard Foster, Jesus was not trying to teach us how to get into heaven, but he was trying to teach how to get heaven into us. Heaven is our ultimate destination, but the daily goal of the Christian is to live as a citizen of the kingdom of God here and now - even during turbulent times. The Bible says *"You have made known to me the path of life; you will fill me with joy in your presence, with eternal pleasures at your right hand."* (Psalm 16:11)

Our faith is strengthened when we understand this:

> *The dark threads are as needful,*
> *In the Master's hand,*
> *As the threads of gold and silver,*
> *In the pattern He has planned.*

A TIME FOR RISKING

"I am with you always, to the very end of the age."
(Matthew 28:20)

It's winter in Texas and as I look out my kitchen window I see native post oak trees bare of their leaves. A fat, lively squirrel runs up the trunk of a tree to the very highest branch. There he stops to contemplate the jump from his perch to the branches of another tree not far away. If he misses the new branch, it's a long fall to the ground. But after a moment he springs into the air. I catch my breath as I see him land ever so lightly on the top branch of the adjacent tree.

I wonder what the squirrel is thinking. Did he take a risk jumping from one tree to another so high up in the air? Or is it his nature to jump from one tree to another without a thought of the dangers?

Then I think of my own Christian experience. Do I take risks for my faith? Am I so warm and secure where I am that I resist going on to some other place? Do I worry so much about the dangers that I'm paralyzed to try anything new?

As I look back on our experience of leaving the warm and loving fellowship of Tallowood Baptist church in Houston to accept a new pastorate in a distant state, I could only think of the loss of familiarity of place and friendships. I worried about how different it would be to serve a church in the southeast. Would I adjust to a new culture and new people? We would be leaving family in Texas who were growing older. Our children would probably go to southeastern colleges, marry southeasterners, and forget their Texas roots. Sometimes it brought me to tears!

Funny, isn't it how such mundane anxieties discourage us from taking risks? Russell has often laughed and said there are two ruts from Texas to Georgia as he "dragged" me to our new place of serving the Lord. But is it really a RISK?

I always appreciated John Bisango who came to First Baptist Church in Houston in the early 1970's. This was my "home" church where I accepted Christ as a young girl and grew spiritually through my college years. My mother was still an active member there. I loved the church.

John left a fast-growing congregation in Oklahoma to come to Houston where my church was experiencing declining attendance and increasing discouragement. Did John consider the move a risk? When others in the Lord's service take up new responsibilities, do they consider that a risk?

Our models in Scripture were risk-takers - people like Esther, Hannah, and Mary, the mother of Jesus. We could name many more as we look through Christian history. There are other women in more recent times like Charlotte Moon of Virginia who took "risks" for their faith.

Webster's dictionary defines "risk" as the "exposure to loss and injury." But a Christian woman, who looks at the task ahead and, in spite of the potential dangers, marches forward with the knowledge that the Lord is with her operates from a more positive definition. Any fear of risks is overcome by the joy and fulfillment of adding to the Kingdom of God.

Miriam Adeney in her book, A *Time for Risking*, admonishes women to follow the example of heroes like Esther and to "risk" using their gifts and talents for Christ in new ways.

The beginning of this 21st century offers a great opportunity for taking risks for Christ. Like that squirrel scrambling up a tree, glancing furtively at the adjacent tree, then taking a "leap of faith," to land safely, we too can take our risks. And we have confidence that we'll land safely, because God has said, *"I am with you always, to the very end of the age."* (Matt. 28:20)

BE SURE TO SEE THE BLUEBIRDS

*"Be strong and take heart, all you who hope in the
Lord."*
(Psalms 31:24)

It was a cold, rainy February day in Houston; and I was confined in my home with three children, ages three, five, and seven with chicken pox! We had been "cooped up" for three weeks as the disease passed from one child to another.

This was before the prevention vaccine and before I had met Sue Sloan. She told me years later that the only way she had gotten through the childhood diseases with seven children was to expose all of them quickly. So she had them all sleep with the one infected, and she had them all drink from the same glass!

From my smallpox "confinement," I telephoned a friend that I was unable to do what we had planned because the third child was now sick. As the three children and I looked out the large bay window of our den into the muddy backyard, I tried to find something interesting to show them.

Suddenly two blue birds - not blue jays - but bluebirds flew to a rain puddle in the middle of the yard. Squealing with delight at their colorful beauty, we began to talk all at once about bluebirds in our own back yard!

We remembered how Judy Garland sang that favorite "Over the Rainbow" from *The Wizard of Oz*.

Somewhere over the rainbow way up high
There's a land that I've heard of, once in a lullaby....
Somewhere over the rainbow, bluebirds fly
Birds fly over the rainbow, why, then, oh,
why can't I?

My children and grandchildren have watched that movie over and over. They've held the book in grimy, little hands and even slept with it. They had to have the doll, Dorothy or the dog, Toto.

Sometimes a young mother feels trapped by the lack of freedom and the constant caring for a family. The drudgery has a way of blinding us to the bluebirds that unexpectedly appear in a busy day. We lose sight of the importance of the child's worth and potential. We scramble for more time for ourselves, or we want to be out contributing to the "real world."

Chuck Swindoll compares life to a combination of multiple seasons with variety, peaks and valleys, change and color. How often we as mothers move through this season of young children without realizing its ultimate purpose of loving, teaching, making memories, and establishing deep spiritual values.

Susanna Wesley was the mother of famous sons John Wesley, the great preacher of the Methodist Church, and Charles Wesley, the author of some 5000 hymns. She wrote in a letter to her husband that she could not but look upon every child under her care as a talent committed to her trust by the great Lord of all families.

That magic moment of seeing the bluebirds was like a sign to me - a reminder that the days of childhood illness which cause anxiety, physical tiredness, and even depression would pass. There really are bluebirds of joy and delight in our backyard if we will only stop and see them.

CHECKING UP

*"Examine yourselves to see whether you are in the
faith; test yourselves!"*
(2 Corinthians 13:5)

Many years ago I read the story of a young boy who entered a drugstore and went into a telephone booth. The door was ajar and the clerk overheard one side of the conversation.

"Is this the company that advertised for help a few days ago?" "Oh, the job has already been filled, has it?" "Does the person who got the job do his work to suit you? Thank you. Good bye."

As the boy came out of the phone booth, the clerk said to him, "Tough luck that you missed out on that job." "Oh, I didn't miss out," said the boy, "I landed that job three days ago. I'm just checking up on myself."

In this day of diet programs and of counting calories, each of us is conscious of her physical weight and fitness. We're flooded with best-selling books on diets, cholesterol, exercise, and the importance of anti-oxidants.

Psychologists today tell us that our society has made self-concern the ultimate goal. We've turned away from the social concerns of the past decades and have focused on self-improvement. Our society has changed from compulsively taking care of other persons to an equally compulsive interest in taking care of self.

Open almost any magazine and you'll find questionnaires rating your intellect, marriage, word power, athletic ability, and fitness. But what about your spiritual strength and fitness?

A rich young man came to Jesus asking what he should do to experience eternal life. Jesus reminded him of the commandments by naming them. To which the young ruler responded, "All these things I have kept from my youth up; what lack I yet?" This man was "checking up." But his concern was his spiritual fitness.

How do we check up on our spiritual health? In 2 Corinthians 13:5, Paul says, "Test yourself, examine yourself, lest you fail the test." A spiritual checkup could include such test questions as:

1. Do I study the Bible more now than I did a year ago?
2. Do I pray more consistently?
3. Am I more regular in my church worship?
4. Do I have a deeper concern for those who do not know Christ as their Savior?
5. Am I using my talents and abilities in my church more effectively?
6. Am I Christ-like in my manner and words?
7. Do I feel gratitude for what Christ has done for me and express it to Him?
8. Do I show my faith is strong when troubles enter my life?

Unlike physical fitness tests, the answers we give to these questions have eternal consequences! Knowing how dangerous a defective compass can be, a good sailor checks its accuracy before embarking on a journey. In our journey of life, we must be sure our compass is accurate. So let's check up on our spiritual health to be sure we're headed in the right direction.

DO WE HAVE TO GO TO CHURCH?

*"Let us not give up meeting together, as some are
in the habit of doing, but let us encourage one
another..."*
(Hebrews 10:25)

I'm sure many mothers have heard this question from their children some time in their lives, "Mom, do we have to go to church? Events can happen at church that make a child not want to go. It might be a bullying child or a sarcastic teacher. Maybe a neighbor who makes fun of people who go to church discourages your children's desire to be a part of their church.

I recall a young mother who began having difficulty getting her five-year-old son to go to church. He had always enjoyed his class but for several Sundays she was actually chasing him around the church halls to get him to go to his class. Not understanding his sudden change, she talked with his teachers. It seems that one Sunday, without her knowledge, her son had brought with him to church one of his toy Peter Pan swords. Not realizing what effect his words would have on a little boy, one of the men teachers scolded him for bringing a "weapon" to church. When the pastor heard what had happened, he eased the tension by asking the little boy one Wednesday night if he had a sword he could use in the pulpit Sunday to illustrate his sermon on David and Goliath!

On Sunday the little boy proudly brought several swords from his collection for his pastor to use, but his mother was able to help her son know that bringing his toys to church was not such a good idea!

Church has always been the unifying force of our family. Attendance and participation helped us flesh out the command, *"Seek ye first the kingdom of God and His righteousness."*

(Matthew 6:33) Now, faith isn't church attendance. But children need external or visual concepts of spiritual truths. Just as they were taught to brush their teeth, to chew food with their mouth closed, and not to interrupt another when speaking, they also need to learn spiritual habits.

Our three went to Sunday school, vacation Bible school, missions, and graded choir activities; and at four years of age, they came into Big Church for worship. These things we just did had started out as rote activities.

But as they grew older, our children understood that these activities were part of their life, and they enjoyed them. Their Christian leaders and teachers helped us teach the concept of the church as a unifying force of the family. Most of all they taught them the way of salvation. So working together with other Christians, we prepared our children to make their own decision to accept Christ as their Savior and Lord.

I recall visiting a Sunday school class member who had become irregular in Bible study and worship. She was the sister of a missionary and had been faithful for many years, but since her children were now grown and away from home in college, she felt she no longer needed to be regular in church attendance.

The last year and a half of my mother's life she moved from the city where she'd lived and the church that she'd attended for 70 years. Her first Sunday in the new setting in Fort Worth, she said to us, "Well, a good Baptist joins a church in the city where she lives, so Russell, if you'll walk to the front with me this morning, I'll move my membership."

During the last six months of her life, when she was unable to attend services, she was ministered to by the pastor and faithful church members. They came to pray and to bring her sermon tapes from the services she missed. Occasionally, as she and I would be sitting on the front porch, the pastor would drive by. When he saw us, he would stop, come up on the porch and encourage her (and me) with his cheerful conversation and laughter.

Whether we're children or seniors, corporate worship – "the assembling of ourselves together" - always brings eternal benefits. We *DO* have to go to church!

GOD HONORS A WILLING SECOND FIDDLE

"Each one should use whatever gift he has
received to serve others,
faithfully administering God's grace in its
various forms."
(I Peter 4:10)

The church orchestra had just finished playing a beautiful arrangement of "Great is thy Faithfulness," and the part played by the strings was exceptional. No wonder the response from the congregation was an audible sigh. All the church members knew the popular, blond college music major who was "first chair" violinist in the string section, but most didn't know the tall, quiet young man who also played violin in the orchestra, and who rose from his chair and went to the podium to play a solo during the offertory. Before playing, he shared a brief testimony that began with the words "God honors a willing second fiddle."

There's such urgency today to be at the "top" of everything that's done. It seems everybody wants to be first. There's not much room to be "second." It's not popular to be an enabler; everyone wants the spotlight.

But what's wrong with being "second fiddle?" I admired this young violinist's attitude. Music was his hobby. He had studied violin for many years, but his profession was in education. He practiced and was faithful at all the orchestra rehearsals, but he would never be "first chair." Nevertheless, he offered his talent to the Lord with a willing spirit.

Some of our talents are "second fiddle." We may have limited ability in music, teaching, decorating, speaking, and other areas, but the Lord asks us to willingly use the talents we do have to further His Kingdom.

So don't be ashamed to be "a second fiddle." When we join with others who are "second fiddles," we can make beautiful music for the glory of God.

GOD'S SPEED LIMITS

"He who listens to life-giving rebuke will be at
home among the wise."
(Proverbs 15:31)

I saw a car ahead of me on the side of the road with blinking red and blue emergency lights. Even though I didn't think I was exceeding the speed limit or breaking the law in any other way, I quickly stepped on the brakes. Seeing the police car, I unconsciously felt I might be guilty.

How much good could be done and how much trouble could be averted if each time we remembered one of God's warnings, we would unconsciously or automatically "put on the brakes?"

We see a lot of television news stories these days about police car chases. A policeman spots a lawbreaker and speeds after the offender. But the person who broke the law doesn't stop when he sees the blinking light of the police car behind him. Instead, he speeds up, going as fast as 90 miles an hour, swerving in and out of traffic, changing lanes, even driving on the shoulder of the road in an attempt to escape the pursuing policeman. All of this endangers the driver, the pursuer, and those around them. Many times, crashes occur, maybe even killing the driver and injuring the policeman and innocent by-standers.

The Bible is our guide book, but sometimes we ignore its teachings, thinking we can get away from the Law. When we occasionally escape without any punishment, we boldly assume we can continue to ignore the Guide. But, like the police chase, trying to escape after a warning sign is given, can lead to your own destruction and harm to others.

God's Word not only advises us about how to live, but like the flashing emergency lights on a patrol car, it also warns us of the dangers of breaking His laws. If we listen and obey God's counsel and warnings, He promises us a full and meaningful life. *"Do not let this book of the law depart from your mouth, meditate on it day and night, so that you may be careful to do everything written in it. Then you will be prosperous and successful."* (Joshua 1:8)

When you see the flashing lights of God's warnings, "put on the brakes." It's dangerous and futile to run from God! The Bible warns us about this kind of car chase: *"Where can I go from your spirit? Where can I flee from your presence?" "For the eyes of the Lord range throughout the earth..."* (Psalms 139:7 & 2 Chronicles 16:9)

I DON'T UNDERSTAND

"He is the Rock, His works are perfect, and all
his ways are just.
A faithful God who does no wrong..."
(Deuteronomy 32:4)

I went for my annual checkup with my dentist who was a dedicated Christian and faithful member of a Baptist church in Fort Worth. He was friendly, warm, and personable.

He endeared himself to me many years ago, not only because of his professional ability but also because of an experience with our son. Robert was a seminary student, and on the previous Sunday he had joined my dentist's church. On the following Wednesday night, as Robert went through the cafeteria line at the church, he heard some one say, "Hey, Robert, it's good to see you tonight."

Robert looked up into the smiling face of Dr. Hodges who was helping serve the plates that evening. Later Robert expressed his feeling that the greeting from Dr. Hodges had made him feel he was at home. He belonged. He felt a part of the church. It was like his home church when his Dad was his pastor.

Well, this wonderful man was unable to retire because of the pressing financial needs of his wife. You see, his lovely wife who was an accomplished pianist had Alzheimer's and needed constant attention.

On the morning of my visit, Dr. Hodges said a little wistfully, "You know, it's funny. A man works hard all of his life and looks forward to retirement so he can do the things he wants with his wife, but circumstances keep him from retiring."

I found myself saying, "I know. It doesn't seem fair, does it?" His response was, "No, but you just do what you have to do and go on trusting God."

Sometimes human experience makes us question God's divine justice. We see evil people prospering and good people suffering. The rule of God does not appear to be just. Those who lead sinful lives are not always punished, and the righteous frequently seem to go unrewarded.

In Psalm 73, David reflects on the prosperity of the wicked. They seem healthy and apparently free from the troubles others experience. This apparent inequity may go on for years, and we find ourselves agreeing with the observation of the Psalmist. How can a just God allow this?

We know that God is just. The Bible tells us so. *"I am the Lord who exercises loving kindness, justice and righteousness on earth; for in these I delight."* (Jeremiah 9:24) We know God is a unified, integrated being whose personality is a harmonious whole, and justness is one of His attributes along with holiness, goodness, love, and truth. It's part of His nature. God cannot be unjust. Because of His holiness, He wants to make things right. Because He is just, He does not show favoritism or partiality. How then can God be both loving and just? On the one hand God's justice seems so severe, requiring the death of those who sin. This seems so fierce, so harsh. On the other hand God is merciful, gracious, forgiving, long-suffering. Are these two sets of traits in conflict with one another?

Actually love and justice have worked together in God's dealing with sinful humanity from the very beginning. God's justice requires that there be payment of the penalty for sin. God's love, however, wants sinners to be restored to fellowship with Him.

The Bible also tells us God is willing to sacrifice to make things right with His creation. He offered his son to be crucified, killed, as the payment for their sin. God so loved the world that He gave His only begotten son that whosoever believes in Him shall not perish but have ever lasting life. The offer of Christ as atonement shows a greater love for us than would the act of simply releasing people from the consequences of sin. *"God demonstrates His own love for us in this: While we were still sinners, Christ died for us."* (Romans 5:8)

During family devotions, Martin Luther once read the account in Genesis 22 of Abraham offering Isaac on the altar. His wife, Katie, said, "I do not believe it. God would not have treated his son like that." "But Katie," Luther replied, "He did."

We know God is just because His story is not yet over. We know that God will ultimately triumph over all evil and His kingdom will reign. Jeremiah 1:8 says *"I am with you and will rescue you to deliver you, declares the Lord."* Romans 4:21 says, *"We are fully persuaded that God has power to do what he had promised."* It is our faith, trust, and hope in Jesus Christ that lets us experience God's justice and His love.

In *My Utmost for His Highest*, Oswald Chambers writes that the Sermon on the Mount indicates that when we are disciples of Jesus Christ there is no time to stand up for ourselves and worry whether we are being justly dealt with or not.

If we look for justice on earth, we will begin to indulge in self-pity, and will waver in our devotion to Christ. We begin to ask ourselves, "Why should I be treated like this?" Jesus tells us to go steadily on with what He has told you to do, and He will guard our life. We must lean not upon our own understanding, but in all our ways acknowledge Him, and He will direct our path.

And so my friend, Dr. Hodges, who didn't understand how love and justice go together, held on to his faith and hope by saying in the midst of life's trials, "You just do what you have to do and keep on trusting God."

I'VE BEEN HERE BEFORE

*"Though I walk in the midst of trouble, you will
preserve my life; you stretch out your hand against
the anger of my foes, with your right hand you will
save me."*
(Psalms 138:7)

One sunny morning in the mid-sixties I drove down
Memorial Drive in Houston to visit a prospect for our
church. As I drove into the new Sandalwood subdivision I
had the strangest feeling that I had been in this area before
that morning. And yet I couldn't remember making any visits
in this area. As I steered the car around the winding streets,
looking for the particular street where the prospect lived, a
large white colonial house came into view.

That strange feeling came over me again. I had been here
before! But when? The house looked so familiar but also
different.

Then, slowly the answer came to mind. This area had
once been owned by a wealthy man and woman whom our
family had known when I was a child. During my college
years I had come to this house with my mother for an
afternoon tea. The gracious hostess was honoring a church
friend who was moving to another city. At that time the house
was surrounded by a large undeveloped wooded area, and a
long winding drive led to the house.

Now the colonial home stood in the midst of smaller
residential lots with houses all up and down the street. The
big white house had remained, but the owner had sold the
surrounding land to be developed into a large subdivision.

This feeling of having experienced some event or place
earlier is called *déjà vu*. Perhaps you've had this feeling. It's
a peculiar sensation, but it also brings a sense of warmth,
remembrance, and joy.

It's so easy to forget the presence of the Lord when you're in the midst of some current crisis. Even though you know Jesus said He would be with you always, many times you're so engulfed with the situation that you think you're all alone.

And yet, something will remind you! In an instance, you remember an earlier occasion when the situation was similar, and the Lord was with you then. Now with the joy of remembering, you *know* He is with you now!

That *deja vu* feeling that you've been this way before, gives you confidence that He is with you now and always.

JESUS IS EVERYWHERE

"Then the Lord spoke to you out of the fire. You
heard the sound of words, but you saw no form;
there was only a voice."
(Deuteronomy 4:12)

There are times in our lives when we badly want to hear a word from the Lord. Usually we go around in our busy lives unaware of God's presence, but when tragedy hits us or we need guidance in an extremely hard decision we go to Him in prayer. The quietness of these prayer times helps us hear God better. We tune out the busy signals of daily life and concentrate on hearing Him.

But we forget that God speaks to us in many other ways. God speaks as we round the turn in the highway and suddenly the field on our left has become a sea of beautiful bluebonnets. He also speaks as the Texas sunset illuminates the entire western sky. God not only speaks in prayer and in nature, but God also speaks in the comments of our children.

As a young mother, I learned to always take my children to the restroom between Sunday school and the church worship service. It was automatic, so that when we were seated in the church auditorium, there would be no asking to go in the middle of the service. When I became a grandmother, I resumed this pattern with my grandchildren.

One particular Sunday, I asked my four-year-old granddaughter to go with me to the restroom. This was my "clever" psychological way of getting her to stop by the restroom, even if she didn't think she needed to. However, on this particular Sunday morning, she was determined not to go. Even when I insisted, and she accompanied me to the ladies' room, she refused to go with me into the stall. I decided to use another "clever" approach and said something like,

"But Nana's afraid to go by herself." She responded, "Nana, don't be afraid! Don't you know Jesus is everywhere?"

If in the busy course of the Sunday, I had forgotten this important thought, a four-year-old granddaughter reminded me. Thank you, Lord, for simple, but profound truths that come from the mouth of a child.

It happened again when my five-year-old grandson was riding with me to the grocery store one day. Unexpectedly, he asked, "Nana, Have you ever seen a dead person?" The question surprised me, but I answered, "Yes, I have." Then he asked, "Do you know what happens to a person when he dies?" Wanting to know what he would say, I answered, "No, I don't." "Well," he said, "When someone dies, it is like walking through a dark alley. He can't see anything. He is alone and lost. But if that person knows Jesus, he has a lighted candle and the light from the candle shows him how to get through the dark alley and Jesus is waiting for him at the end of it." He looked up at me proudly as if to say, "Now you know."

His simple but true explanation touched me, and I asked him, "Who told you that?" "My daddy," he said, matter-of-factly. In that moment God eased any fears I might have had about the level of Christian training my grandson was receiving from his parents.

It is reassuring to remember that God is present with us every minute of the day, and we should not be surprised when He speaks through the voices of our children and grandchildren. Truly, Jesus is everywhere for He said, "I am with you always," and even when we walk through the valley of the shadow of death – or the "dark alley" as my grandson called it - He who is the Light of the world walks with us and leads us into the eternal life beyond.

LIFE ON EASY STREET

*"For everything that was written in the past was
written to teach us, so that through endurance and
the encouragement of the Scriptures we might
have hope."*
(Romans 15:4)

I was reading a local newspaper sometime ago when a headline leaped out at me. In large black letters it said, "Life on Easy Street." It caught my attention because in our complex society we're confronted by difficult circumstances and pressures, and we're all looking for an "easy street."

Quickly my eyes shifted to the article under the headline. As I read, I learned that tucked away inside a large hospital in Dallas, Texas, there is a make-believe neighborhood called Easy Street. It resembles a movie set with streets and curbs, concrete sidewalks, traffic lights, steps to navigate, and big doors to push open. It's a place where patients with short or long-term disabilities practice and rehearse for coping with life outside the hospital.

On Easy Street patients recovering from a stroke or other debilitating illness can re-learn, in a safe environment, how to shop at the grocery store, pull off the plastic sack and open it with only one arm, how to scoot across the bench in a restaurant booth, or how to use a walker on a slippery tile floor. Patients can practice getting in and out of a car with a cane or from a wheel chair. This rehab environment helps patients become self reliant and less fearful when they leave the hospital and are on their own.

In some ways, the Bible is like a "virtual easy street," to help us re-learn some basic elements of the Christian walk when we've been debilitated by hard times. The Bible tells us about people who faced challenges but who remembered and believed God's word, and learned to walk through their hard times as though they were on "Easy Street."

Moses was disappointed when he was not allowed to enter the promised land. However, he didn't become bitter, despondent, or depressed when the final chapter of his life didn't work out as he wanted it to. By trusting God, he found his rough road was actually "Easy Street." The Scripture says, *"Moses was one hundred and* twenty *years old when he died, yet his eyes were not weak nor his strength gone."* (Deuteronomy 34:7)

In the same way, David handled the disappointment of not being allowed to build the temple in Jerusalem, and with a commendable positive attitude he responded to God, *"How great you are, O Sovereign Lord! There is no one like you and there is no god but you...."* (2 Samuel 7:22) Enabled by God's presence, David walked on Easy Street.

Habakkuk couldn't understand why God let the Babylonians, a nation more wicked than Israel, conquer and destroy Judah. But the prophet found his way through his despair and said, *"I will be joyful in God my Savior. The Sovereign Lord is my strength; He makes my feet like the feet of a deer, he enables me to go on the heights.."* (Habakkuk 3:18-19) He had learned how to transform a hard road into "Easy Street."

Every generation encounters disappointment, loneliness, rejection, desertion, fear, and failure along the journey. Because we're human we wish our road was easier, free from hurts and pain. But if we're Christians we remember God's promises in His word. He didn't promise to take away the hurts and pains, but to walk with us so that with His help we can overcome those challenges. Don't forget. Satan was defeated at Calvary on that first Easter morning, and God promised to make us more than conquerors in the midst of life's troubles. When He walks with us, even the most difficult road becomes "Easy Street."

MENTORS

"The mouth of the righteous man utters wisdom,
and his tongue speaks what is just.
The law of his God is in his heart…."
(Psalm 37:30)

It has become popular in today's culture, to have a mentor. Webster defines a mentor as "one who is a wise and faithful counselor." The right mentor can help one succeed in business, in athletics, as a wife and a parent, or in maintaining good health. But perhaps a mentor is most effective in maintaining good spiritual health. Obviously, there are times when you intentionally choose a mentor and they agree to help, but many times, people mentor you without their knowing it. Looking back, I think I've had a number of mentors who didn't know it.

When I was three weeks old, I began a relationship with "Ma Bryan," the nursery worker in Houston's First Baptist church where my parents took me. Ma Bryan was a doctor's wife and the mother of three. She was a tall, rawboned woman with long hair that fell past her waist. She braided her hair and wrapped it around her head.

Later, when I was a teenager, she was the house mother of the big, rambling, two-story frame house each summer at our church camp at Palacios, Texas. She called all of us teenagers, "her girls." She laughed and cried with us over summer romances, but we all knew that along with her sense of humor and fun, her rules as to "rest time" and curfews were absolute. She was caring, practical, optimistic, wise, and enthusiastic. I saw in her the fruit of the Holy Spirit – joy, peace, patience, gentleness, goodness, and faith; and I wanted to imitate her.

I had another "unknowing" mentor when I was a four and five-year-old Sunbeam. I raised my voice as loudly as all the other "beamers" when we sang:

*Wide, wide as the ocean, High as the heavens
    above,
Deep, deep as the deepest sea is my Savior's love.
I though so unworthy, still am a child of His care,
For His word teaches me that His love reaches me,
Everywhere!*

What encouraging theology!

I learned this from Mrs. David Lockard, my Sunbeam leader, whose father, William David Lockard, had been a missionary in Lagos, Nigeria. She also taught me that Jesus loved not only me but the whole world and it was my job to tell them.

My two pastors, Dr. E.D. Head who led me to understand John 3:16 and baptized me, and Dr. Boyd Hunt who made faith meaningful in my teenage years, both unknowingly shaped my life. Dedicated people in the churches where my husband was pastor – people such as Mack and Eunice Roberts at Antelope, Mrs. Buck and Mrs. Fortson at Clifton, Mrs. Crossman and Mrs. Fielder, former missionaries in Houston, the Arthur Rutledges, and Ben and Gretchen Brady in Atlanta - all were mentors to me and probably never knew it.

During our years at Southwestern, I was surrounded by committed faculty and their spouses and many gifted and dedicated students all of whom helped me to grow in faith.

God continues to put in my path wise and faithful Christians who are a source of strength to me and to others, and I am grateful. Have you remembered and given thanks lately for your mentors of yesterday? Have you noticed those today who influence you? They're there even if they don't realize they're your mentors. Be thankful God places them in your life.

OPTIMISTIC OR PESSIMISTIC?

"And we know that in all things, God works for the
good of those who love him,
who have been called according to his purpose."
(Romans 8:28)

Some people are naturally optimistic. They're born with the ability to see some good in everything. Not me! If I have a pain in any area of my body, I'm convinced it's a terminal disease. When a child stuck a nail in her foot or broke an arm, I scolded myself because I had let them go barefoot or climb a tree. I would say "I should have…" and would never think how much worse the accident could have been.

Deanna Harrison in her book, *My Ducks are Really Swans,* says that it's hard for us to distinguish ducks from swans, and that we must take a second or third glance. At first glance a situation appears boring, hopeless, or even tragic. But take a second look, and the event becomes one that God uses to strengthen our character and our faith.

The Faith Sunday School Class of Tallowood Baptist church, composed of women in their 80's, gave me a little book called *Apples of Gold.* In it are sayings like, "no man ever injured his eyesight by looking on the bright side of things," "if you keep a green bough in your heart, a singing bird will come;" and "the blue of heaven is larger than the clouds."

Fortunately, I've lived with a husband for 50 years who is probably one of the most optimistic persons in the world. He has always believed there is good in everyone and every situation. He believes that God is in control and he has lived by the scripture in Romans 8:28." When I would "lose heart" he would say to me that I had forgotten the theology of the resurrection.

Do you naturally have a negative or pessimistic personality? Do you see the hole and never see the doughnut? Is the glass of water half empty instead of half full?

If you have a negative view of life and are discontented much of the time, perhaps this discontentment comes because of a negative feeling about yourself. Usually people are not wanting to make another feel bad. It is how you respond to the treatment someone gives you. Many times you have misunderstood some words. You have seen a hidden meaning in the words which were never intended by the speaker. Psychologists say that we can change our reaction, simply by saying, "Today is a bad day, tomorrow will be better." Sometimes discontentment is part of a personality because the person is focused on herself.

I believe the first step toward living with contentment is cultivating a grateful heart. Stop and look at your life and how you have been blessed. Write down these blessings. Sybil Armes in her book, *Devotions from a Grateful Heart* says that an attitude of thankfulness is the candle of the human spirit for it warms the heart and illumines the countenance. Your face glows and it is not from a new makeup you're trying. This radiance makes others want to be your friend.

Remember past occasions which brought contentment – a birthday party, a trip, a school function, or a reunion with a long time friend. Look at the present and begin today to be content. "Don't wait for some rapture that's future and far; but begin to be joyous, begin to be glad, and soon you'll forget that you ever were sad." This is from my *Apples of Gold* book.

So with the help of my friends, books, my husband, and great promises of God's word I *know* that if you look for the bright side of life, you'll find it.

SAILING

*"When you pass through the waters,
I will be with you;
and when you pass through the rivers,
they will not sweep over you."*
(Isaiah 43:2)

When I was a little girl my mother sang a lullaby to me with these words:

> Baby's boat's the silver moon,
> Sailing in the sky,
> Sailing o'er the deep blue sea,
> While the clouds roll by.
> Sail, baby, sail, out upon life's sea.
> Only, don't forget to sail, back again to me.

When our children and grandchildren were babies, I sang this song to them too.

After speaking to a group of women at my church in which I referred to this lullaby, a friend brought me a children's book in which this song was beautifully illustrated. I'd never seen the lullaby in print, so it was a special gift that meant a lot to me.

Perhaps my enjoyment of sailing stems from that childhood song. I became more familiar with the sport of sailing when we bought a sailboat, and my whole vocabulary broadened. Since I was Russell's "crew of one" I decided I'd better learn the proper terms such as jib, mast, keel, bow, stern, trim, tack, port, and starboard. I also had to learn about the wind, the most important element for sailing.

As we begin the 21st century we'll be sailing through some uncharted waters! We're seeing events in our world that sometimes leave us with little hope and much anxiety.

There are so many problems in our local communities, our nation, and the world: and very few people seem to have any solutions - if there are any.

But with a compass and with some good nautical advice, we can sail through these uncharted waters toward our destination with confidence.

Good sailors know how to anchor the boat safely in a harbor. One fear of a novice sailor is that in a storm, the boat may be blown onto the rocks. The purpose of the anchor is to hold the boat securely in the harbor, even if a gale blows up. When the anchor is in place the boat won't drift out of control.

The Bible tells us we have an anchor to hold our lives steady in this changing and turbulent world, no matter how fierce the storms may be. That anchor is Jesus Christ. How reassuring it must have been to the disciples with Jesus in their boat on the stormy Sea of Galilee. He merely commanded the waves and winds to be still, and they obeyed. (Mark 4: 35-41) It reminds me of two songs:

> "Without Him, I could do nothing,
>   Without Him I'd surely fail,
> Without Him I would be drifting,
>   Like a ship without a sail."
>   And,
> "In times like these, you need a Savior
>   In times like these, you need an anchor
> Be very sure; be very sure,
>   Your anchor holds and grips the solid rock."

A good sailor not only needs to have an anchor, but she needs to catch the wind if she is going anywhere. It is not enough that the wind is blowing. The sailor must pull in the sheets and trim the sails to catch the wind so the boat is propelled through the water.

In the Bible, especially the Old Testament, the Spirit of God is referred to as the "wind." If we are to sail efficiently on life's waves, we must catch the wind, that is, we must depend on the Holy Spirit for power. Just as the wind gives power to the sailboat, so God's Holy Spirit gives power to the Christian. Acts 2:4 tells us that after we repent of our sins and trust in Christ, we receive the gift of the Holy Spirit.

Good sailors need to know how to sail a straight course. Even though a sailor has to turn the helm and sail a zigzag course in order to take full advantage of the wind for power, he must keep his eye on the destination. God wants the very best for us, and He has a plan for our lives. Purpose and meaning become the by-products of a life committed to God and His will for us. Proverbs 3:5- 6 admonishes us *to "Trust in the Lord with all your heart and lean not on your own understanding; in all your ways acknowledge him and He will make your path straight."*

When you're facing rough weather in a sailboat, it's not the time to read the manuals or learn how to sail. In order to cope with heavy weather, a sailor must depend on accumulated knowledge and skills already learned. So it is when we face troubles in our daily living. The reservoir of memorized scripture and the experiences of answered prayer become the help and fortification needed for sailing safely through troubled waters. Do you have a sufficient reservoir of faith to sail through troubled and uncharted waters?

TOUCHING GOD

"People brought all their sick to him,
and begged him
to let the sick just touch the edge of his cloak;
and all who touched him were healed."
(Matthew 14:36)

During a visit to see our redheaded granddaughter, Kelsey, Russell helped her daddy hang a swing in a big tree in their backyard. I could not believe that Kelsey would swing so high. The two chains holding the swing were almost parallel to the ground.

"Higher, higher," she would yell as we took turns pushing her. One particular time when the swing reached its highest point and my heart took a little leap, I heard her squeal, "Oh, oh, I can almost touch the sky."

At that moment I was reminded of the story by Martha Kilgore when another father was swinging his daughter, and she had commanded him to push her higher so she "could touch God." The father asked her if she really thought she could touch God. "Well, I can't right now, Daddy," she answered, "but when I'm as old as you, I'll be able to, and I just want to practice!"

Touching God may be beyond our ability, but feeling His presence in our lives is not. The desire to be near Him and to "touch Him" means we have to spend time with Him. But we have to "practice" with prayer and Bible study and trust. To "touch Him," we need moments of stillness with God to sense His presence.

Tradition says that when the gospel of John was written, the scroll was wrapped in a simple leather cover that bore the likeness of an eagle. The eagle can fly the highest toward the sun, and it builds its nest on the summits of cliffs. Isaiah 40:31 says, "Yet those who hope in the Lord will renew their strength. They will soar on wings like eagles; they will run and not grow weary and they will walk and not be faint." Let's take the time to "touch God," to feel His presence. Let's "soar as eagles," flying so high we can almost touch Him!

YOU NEVER STAND IN LINE

"...In everything by prayer and petition,
with thanksgiving,
Present your requests to God."
(Philippians 4:6)

We were standing on the side of the main thoroughfare in Edinburgh, Scotland. Scores of other people were standing beside us. All of them had come early, and all of them had cameras in hand.

The excitement and anticipation were exhilarating. Queen Elizabeth of England and Prince Philip were scheduled to come down this street in their limousine. Prince Charles was to be in a car behind them.

The cheering and the waving began to build up the street telling us that the royal carriages were coming. As the first one passed in front of us, I stretched my neck and got a glimpse of the Queen in her beautiful blue plumed hat, waving to her subjects. The tall, slender prince consort was at her side. Close on the heels of the first was the carriage with Prince Charles. As they passed we clicked away on our camera, capturing memories of the occasion.

As Christians we have the wonderful privilege of being in the presence of the King of Kings any time we choose. We don't have to stand in line or wait for Him to pass by. He is always present, waiting for us.

Prayer is fellowship with God, our Creator. It is a gift from Him, putting our life at God's disposal and giving Him access to our needs. Prayer honors and glorifies God. It gives Him a channel to work through us to touch the world.

Authentic prayer involves faith and humility, an expectant state of mind and a positive attitude of heart. Prayer is a free, spontaneous communion with God shown in quiet thinking, or in audible words. Its purpose is to mold us in God's image so that we will draw others toward God.

Helen Jean Parks, a long time missionary in Indonesia, says that our prayer requests ought to focus on God's work in the world, asking Him to equip us with the necessary abilities to do His work.

Ruth Graham comments that busy women can cultivate an attitude of prayer all day long. She calls this attitude "praying on the hoof." When you have this attitude it is amazing the Lord coordinates events, people and conversations in ways you couldn't imagine.

As we live life day by day, it's sometimes difficult to see the evidence of God's leadership. We can't see the future, but as we look back, it becomes clear that God's power has been at work in our lives all along. God has loved and cared for us. He has guided, directed, and forgiven us. He has met the physical, emotional, intellectual, and social needs of our lives.

So, prayer is not a choice. It's an obedient and grateful response to God's love and guidance. Remember, we don't have to stand in line. He's always present, waiting for us.

A COMPASS FOR RELATIONSHIPS

FIRST IMPRESSIONS

"Do not judge, or you too will be judged."
(Matthew 7:1)

Have you ever been in a situation where you wanted to make a good first impression but felt you made a rather bad one instead? Recently, since our children were grown and married and our grandchildren were in college, we sold our larger home and moved to a smaller patio home. Back alleys separate the homes and driveways are across from each other.

We had only been in our new home a few days and were anxious to get acquainted with our new neighbors. We had met those on either side of our house, but not the neighbors behind us with whom we shared a back alleyway.

One Sunday morning, probably feeling a little self-righteous that we were one of the few driving out to church, we backed out of our garage into the alley, looking carefully to the right and left. But we didn't look well enough behind us - that is, until we felt a "bump." It was then we realized our neighbor directly behind us was backing out at the same time, and we hadn't seen each other!

Russell quickly jumped out of our car, and our new neighbor stepped out of his. The red reflector on the back of his Cadillac was smashed! Our suburban bumper was not damaged. The two men nervously laughed and confessed they were both guilty. The neighbor quickly assured us his insurance would replace the taillight cover.

Needless to say the next few months I made several visits with cookies to our "back alley" neighbors. We visited frequently at the "accident site" and enjoyed several meals with them. We feel we've corrected our bad first impression and won't be judged too harshly. It did remind us that we shouldn't judge lest be we judged ourselves. And by the way, our neighbors are Baptist and were on the way to their church also that Sunday morning.

A LOST HOME

"The Lord... blesses the home of the righteous."
(Proverbs 3:33)

When I'm asked, "Betty, where are you from? Where is Home?" I always answered that I am from Houston, Texas. I grew up there. I went to Montrose Elementary school, Sidney Lanier Junior High, and Lamar High School. I went with my parents to downtown Houston where we parked the car on Main Street and put a nickel in the parking meter. I believe now the only buildings downtown that remain from my growing up years are the public library (and that's been added on to) and the city hall!

Russell, my husband, has a little harder time distinguishing "where he is from." He was born in Amarillo, Texas in the front bedroom of his grandparents' home on Virginia Street, moved to Port Arthur when he was six, and moved to Wichita Falls when he was 12 years old. Having gone to junior and senior high school in Wichita Falls, he usually says he is from Wichita Falls. (that is, until he meets a person from Amarillo)

When our children were small we were driving through Amarillo on the way to Colorado, and we decided to go by and see the house where Daddy was born. Our youngest child thought this was so exciting – to go see Daddy's "born house." Russell remembered the street and the house number and how to find it. When we arrived at the site, the house was no longer there. A gas service station was built in its place!

Our youngest began crying, "Daddy's born house is gone. Daddy's born house is gone." Months later she would shake her head and mutter those same words, "Daddy's born house is gone."

Sheila Houser is the daughter of Finley and Julia Graham, long time missionaries in Beirut, Lebanon. When Sheila came to Baylor as a student in the 60's, the first question she heard from her new friends was, "Where are you from?" When she replied "Lebanon," someone would inevitably respond, "Lebanon, Texas?"

Sheila has always thought of Beirut, Lebanon as "home," and during her years at Baylor she was often homesick for her home. Some years later, however, when she returned to Lebanon to see the area where she had lived so many years of her life, nothing was there. During many years of war every familiar place to her had been destroyed. Home was no longer there.

So what is home? What does home mean? Among many other definitions, Webster defines a home as "the abiding place of the affections, the abode of one's family, a cheerful, comfortable and friendly place." But in this mobile and changing world, home is no longer a building or even a place.

Sandi Patti sings a song, "Love Shall Be Our Home" that includes the words, "wherever there is laughter, smiles, dreams, singing, and tender hearts there is a home." It is where people can live together in harmony. Home then is where we should first experience love for one another. But if the home is centered in Christ, then that love for others grows out of knowing that God loves us and sent His son to save us and impart his love to us. Roman 5:8 tells us *"God demonstrates His own love for us in this: While we were still sinners, Christ died for us."* It is God's love that we experience in a Christian home, and it is God's love that we show each other. This love is self-giving and constant. No matter what a member of the home does, he or she is loved and forgiven.

So, your home is not a building. It can't be lost. It's anywhere you plant God's love so that the members of that home can be nourished with a love that is personal and will always be there when needs are great. In this 21st century, that's the kind of homes we need.

AFFIRMATION

"A man finds joy in giving an apt reply;
and how good is a timely word."
(Proverbs 15:23)

According to Webster, "affirmation" means "making a positive statement about another person with confidence." When we were at Southwestern Seminary in Fort Worth, a young woman stopped me on the campus and asked if she could talk with me. We arranged to meet the next day, and she poured out her concerns, confessing that her complaints were probably selfish and not appropriate for a true Christian. Her husband had been a successful lawyer in a West Texas town, and she was privileged to be a stay-at-home mother with their two children. They had been very active in their church where she taught Sunday School, sang in the choir, and worked with the mission programs. All the time she served in her church, she was constantly affirmed by the church members. However, her husband began to feel God was calling him to preach, and they had come to the seminary for him to study.

Now, as a seminary student, her husband was pastoring a small church near Fort Worth. She was doing the same things in this church that she had done in their previous church, but there was no affirmation at all from the members. It was more or less expected that as the pastor's wife she should teach Sunday School, sing in the choir, and work with the mission programs. She was having a hard time serving the Lord with gladness, and was hungry for a "timely word" of affirmation.

I understood her feeling only too well, and in trying to lighten her sadness and intensity, I laughingly told her about my own experience. Years before, in our own student church, I had been serving in many of the same ways she had, and I was shocked when a deacon's wife told me that as the pastor's wife, I was not a "permanent fixture." Therefore, according to her, I could not vote on the business presented at the mission meetings.

The lawyer's wife and I read together scriptures that reminded us that our work for the Lord is never void and that our motivation to serve is the praise and glory of God, not the compliments and affirmation of others. As Christian women we know the Bible teaches this, and we feel guilty when we long for human praise. We also admitted that we need to be sensitive to others who need our words of encouragement.

Everybody enjoys a word of praise. In my first public school teaching experience, a wise principal told me that in my parent-child conferences, I should try hard to find something good to say about the child before talking about his problems and shortcomings.

My Dallas friend, Millie Cooper, is one of the best examples of this kind of sensitive encouragement. She has a timely word for everyone with whom she comes in contact. She notices the beautiful eyes of a child and praises her. She sees an unusual pin on the lapel of a waitress and complements her choice. I've learned from her example. She has encouraged me to be more observant and watchful for a timely word I might say to a stranger or a friend.

Let's let Proverbs 15:23 be our compass pointing us to those who need affirming: *"...How good is a timely word."*

ARE OUR HOMES DIFFERENT?

"Let your light shine before men, that they
may see your good deeds
and praise your Father in heaven."
(Matthew 5: 16)

Have you ever asked your child how your home is different from other homes? I have. And her answer was "Well, we go to church a lot; and we don't have any beer in our refrigerator or liquor in a cabinet in the living room."

In today's world a Christian home needs to be more distinct than that. In Isaiah 39 we read about a Jewish king named Hezekiah. In answer to his fervent prayer, God had restored his health and then blessed him with an abundance of material wealth. The passage describes an interesting event that took place while the King was enjoying his good fortune. Some official visitors from Babylon came to see King Hezekiah, and he proudly showed them his wealth and boasted about all the treasures he had accumulated. But apparently he never mentioned that God was the one who had restored his health and blessed him so abundantly.

Later, the prophet Isaiah confronted the King about the foreign visitors who had come to see him. Isaiah asked him a probing question. It's a question for everyone who strives to have a distinctive Christian home. The question was, *"What did they see in your house?" (Isa. 39:4)*

When visitors come to your house, what do they see? Can they tell from a brief visit that your home is different – that you and the family who live in this house are Christians?

During my education classes at Baylor University, I frequently heard my professors say that it's the teacher who sets the atmosphere in her classroom. The excitement and motivation to learn, the desire to be the best student, and calmness under stress are usually the results of a good teacher's example and influence before her students. As parents, we set the atmosphere for our homes. Perhaps there are some things we can do that would let a visitor know we're followers of Christ and that as a result, our homes are different.

For example, a visitor to your home might draw conclusions about how important God's word is to your family by the presence of a Bible beside the bed or on a desk. There might be pictures on the wall of Biblical scenes or framed Scripture passages that lets them know this home seeks guidance from God's word.

Even more important than wall decorations or Bible placement is the relationship between members of the family. In a Christian family, there will be evident concern for each other - parent for parent, parent for child, and child for child. Unavoidable misunderstandings, competition, and harsh words may occur, but they'll happen less frequently and be overcome more quickly if each one is genuinely concerned about the other.

In a Christian home, a parent's attitude toward alcohol, eating habits, exercise, and other issues of good health will set the example for children. A youth minister was confronted by a couple in the church who were shocked that their teenager had been arrested for driving while intoxicated. The youth minister reminded them quite frankly, "You can't expect your child to refrain from drinking alcohol if you have a liquor cabinet in your living room."

Love for the church, and faithful participation in its worship and ministry will have obvious priority in a Christian home. It should be apparent to those who visit such a home that the church and the home are partners in nurturing the family and in proclaiming salvation and spiritual growth to the world.

I visited a young mother of three teen-agers who did not attend church because she thought it was more important to stay home to clean her house and to cook a delicious dinner. As I came into her house and noticed the beautiful decorating, I bubbled over with my complements. Her response was "It's just part of the game, isn't it?" Game? To see how much material gain we can achieve in a short life time? To accumulate lovely possessions and spend time taking care of them? Is that the real game of life? Material possessions aren't sinful, but if the envy and striving for them become the only game of life, and if we teach that philosophy to our children, we're missing the mark in making a Christian home.

My friend, Joanne Leavell, believes that the Christian home is faltering because the "kitchen table" is no longer a center of activity for the family. Eating together as a family is no longer a priority in many homes because busy schedules have displaced family togetherness. Even family activities such as bicycle riding, skiing, hiking, fishing, or running are a challenge to work in to everyone's schedule.

Mary Martin, the beloved stage and screen actress of "Peter Pan," has a quote on the wall of her hometown museum in Weatherford, Texas, "If there is righteousness in the heart, there will be beauty in the character; if there is beauty in the character there is harmony in the home; if there is harmony in the home there is order in the nation."

Is your home different from other homes? Can a visitor sense the difference? Creating and preserving a distinctive Christian home not only blesses the family that lives there, but it also helps bring "order in the nation!"

ARE YOU A FRIEND?

"There is a friend who sticks closer than a brother."
(Proverbs 18:24)

I had been living in Atlanta, Georgia for six weeks. My husband and I and our three children had moved from the pastorate in Houston to a pastorate in Atlanta. Although I knew that it was God's will for us to be there, it was a hard move for me.

One beautiful fall day, I was returning home from taking our children to school. As I drove down the winding street surrounded on both sides by beautiful trees whose leaves were turning gold, red, and orange, the radio broke my reverie with the popular song, "Raindrops Keep Falling on My Head." I was depressed. I was just plain lonely, out of sync with my environment, and just miserable.

Turning into the driveway of our home I noticed the front screen door was ajar. Putting the car into the garage, I went to the front door to see what was obstructing the door. I found a ceramic pumpkin filled with the orange and yellow candy corn found everywhere during the fall of the year. The gift was accompanied with a note that read, "We're so happy that you are in Atlanta. I hope you will love our gorgeous red and gold trees in the fall and our beautiful dogwoods in the spring. Your friend, Margaret Mitchell" And then in parenthesis, "I'm not the one that wrote Gone With The Wind but another Margaret who is hale and hearty."

My miserable spell was quickly broken. I realized afresh how fortunate I was to be in Atlanta and how special our church was to have people who were sensitive to needs and who went out of their way to be a Christian friend.

I pull out that pumpkin from the cabinet every October and place it in the middle of our kitchen table. It not only reminds me of a true friend but it's also a reminder that as a

Christian woman I need to be aware of opportunities to be a friend myself.

We can be a friend intentionally or in unintentional ways. Intentional friendship is realizing someone has a need and responding to that need on purpose like my friend, Margaret Mitchell did.

David Lockard tells of an experience that he had as a missionary in Africa. As he was traveling down a road one day, hurrying to a meeting, he saw a truck broken down on the side of the road. He looked hard at the truck, but thinking he didn't have time to stop, drove by. Then something pricked his conscience. He turned his car around and went back to the broken down truck. As he got out of his car, the occupants of the truck came toward him. He recognized one of them as a member of their congregation. He said, "Oh, Brother Lockard, I told my friend that was your car and that you were a Christian like me and that you would stop and help us." David said how close he came to overlooking an opportunity to share the love and concern of Jesus with someone in need.

Unintentional friendship is a lifestyle of serendipitous surprises. It is important to remember that people count and that interruptions may be unplanned opportunities to be a friend.

As Christian women we're part of the kingdom of God. In one sense the Kingdom of God exists in the future, but in another sense it is present now. It is God's rule over people who believe in Jesus as the Savior and Reconciler of the world. As a citizen of the Kingdom, a Christian is called to further God's rule and represent the Lord Jesus Christ by being a friend indeed to someone who needs your help. This kind of ministry is one of the most convincing proofs of a person's relationship with God. John 13: 35 says *"By this men will know that you are my disciples, if you love one another."*

When we're busy, it's sometimes distracting, costly, and inconvenient to be a friend. At other times we believe the help a person needs is too complicated and beyond our capacity to help. On other occasions the need is so insignificant it hardly seems worth our while to get involved. But the size of the need is not the important thing. It's the act itself. More than likely, we have more opportunities for small services than for larger ones. But because they take little time and energy, we often neglect them. We need sensitivity and awareness to see the need – large or small – and then, refusing to pass by on the other side, to stop and help.

Sometimes becoming a friend requires nothing more than a word or a note of encouragement. We can initiate friendships by inviting guests into our home or in countless ways. All one needs is a sense of timing, genuine sincerity, and sensitive thoughtfulness – like my friend Margaret Mitchell had.

Paul Tournier has written that our lives are an adventure directed by God. Let the adventure of making friends bring joy and satisfaction to your adventure.

ARE YOUR DUCKS ALL IN A ROW?

"...For I have learned to be content whatever
the circumstances."
(Philippians 4:11)

This phrase, "My ducks are all in a row," was a favorite saying of Mrs. Crossman, a retired home missionary, who was a member of our church in Houston. In saying these words, she was inferring "all is well with my soul." Mrs. Crossman lived knowing that nothing could separate her from the love of God which is in Jesus Christ. Her desire was to have a heart so full of joy that life's withering storms could not destroy it.

I took some clothes to the cleaners last week, and since I've been a regular customer for some time, I usually stop to talk with the young woman behind the desk as I leave my clothes. On that particular morning, she said, "My, you sure look happy today. You must be feeling good." I quickly responded, "Yes, I do. I've cleaned out closets this week and gotten some other work done that's been hanging over me to do, and I guess I'd say all my ducks are in a row this morning. As I walked out to the door to her parting "Have a good day," I thought of Mrs. Crossman's saying. Is this what it takes to make me content so that it shows - having all my ducks in a row?

What does it take to keep a smile on our face and radiate joy so that someone notices and asks about our lives? Do we have to have finished chores behind us, good health, affirmation, children who make good grades, a husband who brings us gifts, all the latest technological buttons in our homes?

I teach a Sunday School class of women who are 72-82 years of age. Through these years that we've been together, they've had many ups and downs in their lives, and yet so many of them are examples to me of persons with real joy in their lives. There's a noticeable contentment visible not only to me, but to the young women in our church as well.

For example, there's Maxine, faithful in class and usually sitting by herself in the worship service of the church. A long-time member of the church, she was married to a Jewish man who never came with her to church. In spite of this, she saw that her three children were active in the church and came to know Christ as their Savior. Margaret, Jean, Vinitia, and others who've been recently widowed have shown me that joy can be expressed even in loneliness.

Jesus wants his followers to experience His joy in their lives – a joy that is constant, remaining with us during the good times and the bad. He said, *"These things I have spoken to you, that My joy may be in you, and that your joy may be made full."* (John 15:11) This joy comes when we completely trust in God, and are trying to do His will, knowing with certainty that we will ultimately overcome. Paul must have had this in mind when he prayed for the Christians in Rome, *"May the God of hope fill you with all joy and peace in believing, that you may abound in hope by the power of the Holy Spirit.* (Rom. 15:13)

Carolyn Rhea has written that joy comes only as a dividend. As one gives her life unreservedly into the hands of God, allowing Him to invest it on earth where there is need, then that invested life earns continuous dividends of spiritual joy. Are your ducks all in a row?

BARRIERS

"...No eye has seen, no ear has heard,
no mind has conceived
what God has prepared for them who love him."
(1 Corinthians 2:9)

Our Sunday School class had gone to the Buckner Ranch in the Texas hill country for a week-end retreat. I was sitting in the large rocker on the front porch of the Faith building. The railing at the edge of the porch was right at my eye level, blocking my view of people walking on the sidewalk in front of the building. All I could see were the trees and the sky. That railing was a barrier, preventing me from seeing my friends. Although the soft rocker was very comfortable, I decided to move to the cold, hard steps of the porch so I could see.

There are many barriers in a Christian's life preventing her from seeing people who need her friendship, love, and concern. Sometimes these barriers are cultural and economic. Ruth Senter has acknowledged that barriers to friendships can be such things as disappointment in the other person's actions, competition for attention, or quiet envy over material possessions. Barriers can also be the feeling that the person's need is so great and that helping them would demand too much time. Getting involved threatens the commitments we've already made.

What are the barriers in your life that keep you from seeing others and their needs? Is it a self-centered desire to look out for you? Is it a failure to truly understand that God loves that person in need? When the moon gets between the earth and the sun, we call it an eclipse. When earthly distractions get between you and Christ, it's a spiritual eclipse, and it blocks our view of others in need.

The apostle Paul could never understand how a person who had met Christ would not have an intense desire to reach out to others. Paul knew that the presence of Christ within a believer would remove the barriers that keep us from seeing others. But knowing Jesus personally gives us an added benefit: Jesus also removes the chains of sin that enslave us, and when those sinful barriers come down, the way is open for God to bless us with a full and meaningful life.

DETOURS

"...Patience is better than pride."
(Ecclesiastes 7:8)

One Thanksgiving, we were returning to Fort Worth from Waco, driving north on Interstate 35, a section of highway that is perennially under construction. (Our friend, Landrum Leavell says they'll be working on it 'til the end of time!') Traffic was backed up for miles, and a slow line of cars was edging its way north.

Impulsively, we took an unmarked exit, thinking we could pick our way through the back roads, go around the traffic snarl, and eventually return to the highway home. The side road twisted and curved, and it soon became obvious that we were going farther and farther from our destination. The daylight ended and night began to envelope us, but eventually we wound our way back to the interstate beyond the slow traffic and continued toward Fort Worth at a good pace. Our detour had actually taken more time than we would have spent waiting in the slow-moving traffic!

But during that little excursion, we saw beautiful rolling landscapes, a gorgeous sunset, a full rising moon, and impressive Christmas decorations and lights in the yards of stately country homes – all of which we would have missed if we had stayed on I-35. It was a serendipity experience. Now, on occasions when circumstances make us impatient and discontented, we'll smile at each other and say, "Remember the experience on highway 35!"

Most hard-driving "type A" people – those who make lists at night of "things to do" the next day - become impatient when obstacles prevent them from accomplishing something within a certain time frame. But if they were patient, they might discover that unexpected detours let them experience surprising blessings.

I'm sure the Samaritan traveler on his way to Jerusalem was in a hurry to get to his destination before dark. But he "detoured" to help the Jewish victim of a roadside robbery and found himself the hero of Jesus' parable!

Maybe the possibility of blessings during detours led to God's reprimand to the Children of Israel. In the 21st chapter of Numbers the Lord had led them out of Egypt and helped them win a victory over the Canaanites. But then in order to proceed to the promised land, God told Moses to lead them around the land of Edom. This detour was a much longer route, and the impatient people were anxious to get to their destination, so they rebelled, complaining against God and Moses. The Lord punished them for their complaining, and they eventually repented and took the longer path. Looking back, I'm sure they discovered God had their best interests at heart, and the detour was actually a blessing in disguise.

Someone has said that a determination to accomplish goals is a virtue of well-organized lives. We see the impressive results of that determination in the accomplishments of great musicians, physicians, gymnasts, and other outstanding performers. But what we may not see are the many obstacles these heroic achievers had to overcome in order to meet their goals. Sudden accidents, unexpected illnesses, financial crises, bad weather are only some of the untold interruptions they must have patiently endured. Their patience during detours allowed them to experience the blessings of uncommon accomplishments.

Perhaps patience is even more important when we try to understand and accept the faults and imperfections of others. Thomas a' Kempis said that if you're not able to make yourself what you want to be, how can you expect to mould someone else to what they should be? We need to have patience with our own shortcomings as well as patience with others who have authority over us, with those who don't like us, and most of all, with those who love us.

Scripture commands us to wait on the Lord and reminds us that patience is a gift of the Spirit. Our compass may sometimes point us to a detour, but joy in life comes when we patiently enjoy the unexpected blessings of the side trip.

I WISH I'D KNOWN

"Blessed is the man who finds wisdom, the
man who gains understanding."
(Proverbs 3:13)

Recently, we made a trip to Maine in the fall and enjoyed the beauty of the changing trees with their leaf color, the roaring of the waves and tides on the rocky coastline, the majesty of the white steepled colonial Congregational and Baptist churches, and the loaded abundance of red apples on the trees. The scenery was so different from the environs of my life in Texas.

My father was a boy in Maine and Massachusetts, and he came to Texas when he was about 16 years of age. He died when he was 47 years old, while I was a senior in high school. So I knew very little about my daddy. Erma Bombeck has said that we know less about our parents than any other people with whom we associate. I think she was right.

My father never returned to the northeast after he came to Texas. The responsibilities of finishing his education, finding his vocation, marrying my mother, beginning a family, fulfilling tasks in his church and community organizations, and his early death gave him little time to retrace childhood steps. The economic times of the 20's, 30's, and 40's also gave him little opportunity to vacation very far from Texas.

Daddy was a distinguished-looking person – six feet tall, slender, big brown eyes, a carefully trimmed mustache, a receding hairline at the temple of his slightly graying, dark hair. He was courteous, polite, specific in manners, and expected his children to be obedient. His mother died when he was about eight years old, and later he had a harsh stepmother. His father died just before he and my mother were married. So I had no grandparents to tell me about their life in New England or about my father's boyhood.

My whole understanding of my Dad's life before Texas was a painting of a Boston schooner which hung over the living room mantle and eating Boston baked beans (flavored with molasses), New England boiled dinners (with turnips), and salami and liverwurst sandwiches – none of which I liked.

It never dawned on me that he might have longed to return to his native northeast to see the same beauty that I experienced on my trip. As we played in the puny waves of Galveston beach, I wonder if he ever remembered the majestic, rocky shoreline he knew as a boy. When Houston had a rare spattering of snow - perhaps twice during his years in Texas - I wondered if he recalled sledding with his younger brother in the deep snow of New England.

Many of the things I know now about my Dad came from keepsakes I found in my mother's cedar chest after she passed away. Those items and this recent trip have helped me to understand my father in a way that I never experienced in his lifetime.

It has made me realize anew that circumstances, experiences, and environment shape a person's life; and if we really want to understand and love them more deeply, we need to know their background. This is true of our family members, but it's also true of the people we work with and encounter every day. Sometimes we're so quick to react negatively to criticism, conversations, and actions of someone without really understanding "from whence they have come."

The trip to Maine has given me unforgettable memories of our beautiful country, but it's also reminded me of how I can best understand the people around me – especially my father. I wished I'd known.

ILLUMINATING MOMENTS

"Your word is lamp to my feet, and
a light for my path."
(Psalm 119:105)

When I was in the ninth grade, I took typing as an elective subject. I remember the day I no longer had to look at my hands or the wall chart in front of me to type. I could keep my eyes on the lines in the book and type the words smoothly without looking at my fingers! I said to myself, "So that's how it works!" It was as if the shade on the window of my mind had been raised and the light suddenly came through.

I'm sure all of us have had these illuminating moments when there was a breakthrough of knowledge or performance of a skill. Perhaps it was when we learned to ride a bicycle or to ski a snowy mountain slope. We told ourselves, "I got it!"

I've also found this to be true during Bible study when God breaks through with a new thought, even though we may have read a certain scripture many times. Sometimes this new insight is merely rediscovering a spiritual concept we had forgotten in our busy lives. God knows we need new encouragement from Him at certain times in our lives, and he spotlights that new insight as we read His word.

Some people call these break-throughs "Ah-Ha' moments, and busy lives keep us from having them more frequently. Ruth Graham admitted that spiritual dryness in her life usually followed an extremely busy period. So in the "busyness" of raising five children, she would stop and take time to get refreshed by reading the Bible. Many of us are like Martha of Bethany in the Bible. Inward quietness is hard for us. We'd rather be outside "doing" than inside reading. But there come times when we've given all we can to a task and realize no matter how hard we work, our influence is

71

still ineffective. That's when we need to stop and receive the inspiration we need from our Guide.

Time makes demands on all of us. Circumstances bring unavoidable pressures and stress. But moments of illumination from God's word give us His perspective and power, clarify our priorities, give us calmness and confidence, and change our attitude. Make time for these illuminating "Ah-Ha" moments.

IS THERE A HAPPYVILLE?

"I have told you this so my joy may be in you..."
(John 15:11)

When I was living in Atlanta, Georgia, I became acquainted with a suburb south of Atlanta named Hapeville. One day in the grocery store I overheard two women, evidently uninformed newcomers, discussing the area. One said to the other, "Have you been to Happyville, yet?" Happyville! My, wouldn't it be nice if there were such a place where happiness abounded all the time –a place where all those anxieties, fears, doubts, worries or discouragements that come on us more often than we like to admit would disappear?

The search for happiness is not just today's problem. It's been a desire ever since history began. In the Garden of Eden, Adam and Eve had everything they needed, but they wanted more. Their search for happiness tempted them to eat the fruit from the tree God had declared off limits, and they discovered that trying to live on man's terms, rather than God's can't bring happiness.

In many parts of the world, the bluebird is a symbol of happiness. Residents impatiently wait for the soft, plaintive warble of the bluebirds early in March. Snow may still whiten fields and gardens, high winds still may blow about the trees and chimneys, but the bluebird's persistent song proclaims that spring is coming. W. L. Dawson, a bluebird-lover from Ohio, exclaimed that the bird "reflects heaven from his back and the earth from his breast. He floats between sky and earth like the winged voice of hope."

Bluebirds are found all across America, and the states of Missouri, Ohio, and New York have chosen it as their state bird. In other states there are organized societies to protect the bluebird and increase their population.

Because of its color, some people mistake the larger, noisy, and mischievous blue jay as a bluebird. But the bluebird is a medium-sized bird, about seven inches long, cheerful, and charming, with a quiet, gentle demeanor as it perches. There are interesting variations in the eastern, mountain, and western bluebirds, but usually the females have duller blue wings and a tail, while the males have a bright blue color on top and a reddish brown throat and breast. (Like the sky and the earth!)

I like to compare the bluebird with a Christian woman as a creature of beauty, happiness, and joy – one whose life heralds the springtime of joy and hope. She can be that kind of creature if she lives in the assurance that God is at work for good in all bad situations for those who love Him. Pressures, stress, pain, and disappointments are all part of living, but I think a Christian woman's influence, like the bluebird, can bring a note of hope and joy to brighten the dark days.

Maybe this is why we liked Erma Bombeck and her writings so much. Through humor, she helped us see that the real-life, stressful experiences that frustrate us are merely a normal part of the thread of life. These unfortunate pressures come in many ways and in varying degrees of intensity - unexpected accidents, the loss of loved ones, a financial setback, conflicting relationships, concerns with our children, and caring for elderly relatives. But Bombeck's humor helped us remember that the clue to living in joy is how we react to these "normal" situations. We can let the bad things destroy our joy or we can laugh a little and allow them to develop a wiser and stronger character.

Someone has said that no one ever injured their eyesight by looking on the bright side of things. Maybe there can be a Happyville after all!

IT TAKES MANY

"For everything in the world - the cravings of sinful man, the lust of his eyes, and the boasting of what he has and does - comes not from the Father but from the world."
(1 John 2:16)

It's a beautiful fall day. I'm driving to the church to meet my friend and to pick up the two coolers that contain the "Meals on Wheels" for the clients on our route. It's 8:45 in the morning, and I'm feeling a sense of smug contentment with my life and my activities. After all, I'm taking free meals to elderly, handicapped, needy people. It feels good to hear the grateful compliments of those on my route who are glad to have me help them.

My friend, Martha, and I have been doing this for some time, and I'm proud that even though both of us are busy, we've organized our schedules so that we seldom have to ask for substitutes. As I continue proudly down the road. It suddenly dawns on me that I couldn't be doing this if it weren't for many others who are providing *their* services too.

There is the driver of the delivery truck who brings the coolers to the church by nine o'clock each morning. There are the helpers and the cooks who have packaged and prepared the meals. There are those who have purchased the food from the wholesale companies who have provided their products at reduced prices. There is the organization that funds the purchase of the food. There are the many office helpers who keep the ever-changing list of the names and addresses of those needing the meals and who make sure the route drivers are dependable. There are those who give money so that this organization can continue.

In the light of this realization, my self-centered attitude changes. Humbly, I ask a prayer for all those who are faithfully doing their jobs so that I can do mine. Together we help others.

The Bible, which is our compass for life, tells us that God hates the sins of self sufficiency and pride. So in humbleness of spirit and gratitude for others who clear the way for us to serve, I take new joy in the realization that it does indeed take many!

MOMENTS OF JOY

"May the God of hope fill you with all joy and
peace as you trust in him so that you may overflow
with hope by the power of the Holy Spirit."
(Romans 15:13)

All of us have our moods, our "ups and downs" as we call them. Even the happiest of us go through "down times" of despondency and sadness, but God's word tells us that even the "down times" can be interrupted by moments of joy. C.S. Lewis described these intermittent moments of happiness in the midst of sadness as being "surprised by joy."

In Luke we read how a priest named Zacharias was surprised by joy. For many years, he had led the worship service in the temple at his appointed time, and it had become a routine for him. But one day, as he came into the temple, he was surprised. An angel beside the altar told him he would become a father, even though he and his wife were old. But most surprising of all, this child would be the forerunner who would point Israel to God's Messiah. What an unexpected moment of joy!

One summer our family spent several weeks at Ridgecrest, North Carolina. We drove up to Blowing Rock one evening to eat at a popular restaurant. I wasn't in a very joyful mood, because we were considering the possibility of leaving our great church in my hometown, Houston, Texas to accept a call to an unknown church in Atlanta, Georgia. The future was uncertain. Our long time friend, Jesse Fletcher, who helped appoint Baptist Journeymen and missionaries to foreign countries, was amazed at my reluctance to move to Atlanta. He said, "Betty, I've sent people to the most depressed third-world countries in Africa and Asia that weren't this unhappy!"

After our meal, as we drove back down the Blue Ridge Parkway to Ridgecrest, fog closed in and Russell had to drive very slowly. It had been our custom for many years for our family to sing in the car while traveling. So it was not unexpected when the kids in the back of the Suburban broke out singing, "I See the Moon" (Which, of course because of the fog, we didn't!), "This Land Is my Land," and then the chorus, "Sing, Make a Joyful Sound, Sing, Life in Christ Is Found." In that moment I experienced a sudden inner feeling of joy in a family that could rejoice and sing together, and I knew there was nothing to fear about the future. I was surprised by joy!

Then there was a day when I walked into the educational building of First Baptist Church, Euless, Texas on a Tuesday morning to speak to their women's luncheon group. A young woman came walking toward me in the hallway, and as she recognized me, she stopped and introduced herself. She offered to show me to the meeting room, and as we walked together down the hall, she said, "I want to tell you something important. I accepted Christ as my Savior during a summer tent meeting when your husband was preaching. It was in Wichita Falls, Texas some 25 years ago." I remembered Russell telling me about that summer. The First Baptist there was beginning a new mission, which later became the Faith Baptist Church. The men of the church had put up a tent on the property, and for two weeks, Russell and another young "preacher boy" from Baylor, John Wood, took turns preaching and leading the music.

Later, as I was thinking about this young woman's testimony, I was filled with joy that God had used a young college boy who was preaching his very first sermons after he had felt God calling him to preach. How scared he had been. How hard he had struggled to write those summer sermons. But God had blessed their efforts, and people had responded with public professions of faith and rededications.

Her sharing that experience with me was a serendipitous moment of joy.

Robert Raines calls these fleeting moments of happiness "kissing the joy as it flies." It's the feeling that God is present, and His arms are around us to help us live boldly for Him without fear.

True, these flying flashes of happiness are short lived, but they help us grow toward a more mature level of *always* living in joy. That's what Christ wants for us and what Paul prayed for when he said, "May the God of hope fill you with all joy."

PEBBLES IN A POOL

*"You are the salt of the earth... You are the
light of the world."*
(Matthew 5:13, 14)

All of us have thrown a pebble in a pool of water. We enjoy seeing how the ripple where the pebble hit the water spreads in concentric circles larger and larger out into the water. The influence of a Christian is much like that.

Caitlin, the college freshman daughter of Kathy and Brad Creed, was killed in an automobile accident while driving to see her grandparents in East Texas. What an incredible blow this was to her family and their many friends. The sorority she had pledged in college made a scrapbook of Caitlin's short life. It included comments that pointed to Caitlin's influence as a Christian: "On Sundays, she always called us to encourage us to meet her at church," "Caitlin always gave thanks before eating her meals," and "She knew that whatever God allowed in her life, He would be there with her." Obviously, her life, like the ripples on the water touched many of her contemporaries.

We received a letter from Anne, the daughter of a family who lived next door to us in Houston, some 30 years ago. Anne was a friend of our daughter, Ellen. They rode bicycles together and swam together in the neighborhood pool. When the girls were ten years old, her family moved to California from Houston, and we moved to Atlanta. We had not heard from them in many years. In her letter Anne wrote:

"I remember the evenings I stayed with you when my mom and dad went out. I can also remember attending services at your church. My parents were very fond of you and your children. I want to let you know that I'm 36 years old, happily married to a good Christian man, the mother of two boys, and all of us are active in the Lutheran church. I became a Christian and joined the Lutheran church when I was pregnant with my first child. I am so happy to say that I have a strong Christian marriage and family life."

Anne had hunted up our address from a Baptist pastor in her city in California in order to tell us that her parents had both died of cancer within the last two years. Before their deaths, they had accepted Christ and joined an Episcopalian church in which they had become active.

Because of Anne's letter I felt that in a small way, even though it took a long time, and even though we were not aware, the influence of our home in Houston, like ripples on the water, touched these neighbors and their daughter and encouraged them to develop Christian homes.

Sometimes one's influence on an unbeliever reaps its results quickly, but there are other times when it takes many years for someone to influence another to become a Christian. The good news is that all of us have the potential to be Christ's light in a dark world – like the spreading ripples on the surface of a pond.

RECONNECTING

"Jesus Christ is the same yesterday and today,
and forever."
(Hebrews 13:8)

Growing up in Houston I had a friend named Jeannine who was two years older than I. She was tall, thin, brunette, and had blue eyes. She had all the external attributes that I wanted to have. I was short, prone to pudginess, blonde, and had brown eyes. She could eat a whole pint of ice cream at one time, and it never showed on her slight frame! And her name "Jeannine" was so lovely, not like plain "Betty."

We skated on our sidewalks, rode bicycles, and played monopoly on hot summer days. We talked about our problems with teachers, and other girl friends. We talked about our disappointment in not being chosen for special events and losing ball games. Jeannine was a Methodist and sometimes asked me to go to their Sunday evening youth programs which I would have liked to have done sometimes, but I was a Baptist and went to Training Union!

Jeannine graduated from high school and went to Southern Methodist University in Dallas, and two years later I went to Baylor. So our paths separated.

Fifty years passed and my husband, Russell was preaching on a Sunday morning at Park Cities Baptist Church in Dallas. An attractive, slightly gray-haired woman came towards me after the service and said, "Betty, I go back a LONG way." I looked at her hard, and just as I was about to shout, "Jeannine," she said, I'm Jeannine Frazier Neiman."

Needless to say we quickly sat down and tried to catch up on our lives. Jeannine had married a Baptist, and her daughter and family had been active members of Park Cities Baptist Church for many years. Sometime later Jeannine and her husband moved to a beautiful lake home in North Texas. We were happy to reconnect.

But it didn't end there. A few years later when Russell was serving as interim president of Howard Payne University, a Baptist school in Brownwood, Texas, Jeannine wrote to tell me that her husband was from Brownwood and was an alumnus of Howard Payne. That was another experience of reconnecting!

Have you had that experience of reconnecting with a friend? There is such joy in seeing each other again. You're both talking at once, trying to find out so much that has happened in your lives. You're both bubbling over with excitement and enthusiasm.

When we moved to the suburbs of Houston in the late 1950's to start a new Baptist church, we were invited to dinner one evening by a Presbyterian pastor and his wife. Rodney and Mae Sunday had started a Presbyterian church in the same Memorial Drive area. I was most appreciative of the invitation at the time, but as the years passed I became even more grateful for the thoughtful expression that a fellow pastor and his wife extended towards us, and they were not even Baptists!

Forty-three years later we received a letter from Mae and Rodney Sunday who were now living in the Texas Hill Country. She had seen our name in her neighbor's Howard Payne Alumni Magazine and took the opportunity to write us. In responding to her letter, I explained how often during these past years as I spoke to ministers' wives groups, I would tell them of this heart warming invitation which they had extended to us as new ministers in the "field." I used her as an example to encourage the Baptist ministers' wives to do the same for other new ministers moving into their area. What a joy to reconnect!

RECONNECTING. It's an experience that is possible only with increasing age and the passing of time. As the years go by, circumstances and distance separate us from friends, but reconnecting brings renewed enjoyment and gratitude for that person from your past.

When did you first become a friend of Jesus? When did He become your friend? Have you kept the friendship up to date and vital through 10 years, 40 years, 50 years and even more? He doesn't move away. He doesn't get so interested in others that He is no longer interested in you.

He's truly a friend, and you can take your problems and disappointments to Him now just as easily as you did when you first met Him, and He became your friend and Lord. But are you doing it? I love to sing the old hymn, "What a friend We Have in Jesus," and remember that Jesus Christ is the same yesterday, today and tomorrow.

RECONNECT now.

WHO AM I?

"...Being confident of this, that He who began a
good work in you will carry it on to completion until
the day of Christ Jesus."
(Philippians 1:6)

The twenty-first century has brought us a new threat called "Identity Theft." Every day the news carries another story about it. People are stealing social security numbers, security passwords, and bank account numbers, and then using them to assume the identity of an unsuspecting victim. When this occurs, it often takes years of struggle for the victim to reclaim her rightful identity.

In the childhood classic, *Winnie the Pooh,* Tigger loses his stripes after a good washing. Without his identifying stripes, he doesn't know if he's Tigger or not. He loses not only his self-identity, but his self-confidence as well.

Some of us identify our self-image with a relationship we have with a husband, a daughter, a wife, or mother. For others, the self-image is shaped by her profession or career. In either case, when those relationships or that profession changes, the person may feel like Tigger. She's lost her stripes and her identity.

Insecure people often compensate by assuming a proud, exaggerated self-image that inevitably leads to broken relationships with God and others. Still others look at themselves critically, seeing faults and features they wish weren't there.

Such a low self-esteem leads to a lack of confidence. Bob Brackney, a religious education professor, remembers how his small physical size always distressed him as a young boy. "I'm grown now and only five feet five inches tall. Imagine how I felt back then when my school mates chose the teams for a basketball game!" That's why Mark Twain said that a person can't be comfortable without his own approval.

The Bible tells us that Elizabeth, the mother of John the Baptist, was a victim of low self-esteem. She had no children, but when she opened her life to God, she realized God had a special purpose for her and that He could overcome her limitations and make her life useful. How that must have elevated her self-image!

Peter wrote to the Christians in Asia Minor that they were a chosen generation and a peculiar people because Jesus had called them out of darkness into marvelous light so they could show God's greatness to others by their daily living. How that must have elevated their self-image.

Identity theft is a serious threat today, but even more serious is the problem of "identity depreciation." In 1940 eleven percent of women in the United States felt worthless. In 1980 sixty-six percent of women in our country felt this way. Now in the twenty-first century the percentage is till growing. Self-esteem has become the personal growth issue of this decade.

As a result, enumerable books have appeared, claiming to give us helpful suggestions for raising self-esteem in women. They include making a list of accomplishments along with our weaknesses, trying not to compare yourself with others, forgetting your mistakes and learning from them, overcoming fears, taking an interest in others, recognizing the things that are stressful, and working toward eliminating them. Someone has said, "You grow up the day you have your first real laugh – at yourself." A sense of humor helps to reduce one's feelings of inferiority.

The Bible gives even better advice: *"Let us not become conceited, provoking and envying one another."* (Galatians 5:26) *"For the Lord will be your confidence and will keep your foot from being snared.."* (Proverbs 3:26)

When a Christian woman desires to follow God's will for her life, she – being made in His image - discovers what her Creator intended her to become. Who am I? Since Jesus is the King of Kings and since I belong to Him, I'm a child of the King! That should be your self-image and your identity.

YORKIES ARE SPECIAL

"Perfume and incense bring joy to the heart
and the pleasantness
of one's friend springs from his earnest counsel."
(Proverbs 27:9)

Our daughter has a loving relationship with her Yorkie, "Mason," who is four years old. She cuddles him, watches his diet, lets him sleep at the foot of her bed, and calculates the amount of fresh air he needs each day.

I like dogs, but I've never had that kind of relationship with one. The mixed terrier we had when our children were growing up, usually stayed in the fenced backyard. We built a special place for her in the back of the garage which she could enter through a "doggie door" on cold days and during summer rains. Her three litters of puppies were enjoyed by the whole family, but I was quick to find another home for those puppies! We didn't need more than one pet.

But my daughter and her "Mason" have shown me how friendships can accelerate when dogs are involved. Vicky, one of her co-teachers, called her the other day with tragic news. She was in tears. Her Yorkie had been hit by a car and was killed. The next morning, dropping everything else, our daughter spent the whole day driving Vicky from place to place to find another Yorkie. It was an unselfish act of friendship motivated by a shared love of dogs.

In the hectic, busy schedules we all have today, stopping everything to be a real friend to someone is often overlooked. It's hard to find the proper balance in a Christian life. On the one hand, there's the pressure to finish the things that need to be accomplished at home, with the family, and in your job. But on the other hand there are the problems and needs of others around us whom we care about. Ruth Graham once said that she didn't work well under pressure, but that she didn't work at all without it. That's true, but how do you balance the different pressures that compete for our time?

When we see needs around us everywhere we become frustrated and confused. It's a continual battle not to become overcommitted. To say, "I can't do it all" is not a good excuse to avoid being a friend to someone in need.

Our lives are an adventure directed by God. But a vital part of that adventure is nurturing friendships. That brings joy and satisfaction not only to the one to whom you are ministering, but also to you. Let your inner spiritual compass guide you to balance the pressures of the adventure so you don't miss the double blessings of ministering relationships.

FRIENDSHIPS

"I tell you the truth, whatever you did for
one of the least
of these brothers of mine, you did for me."
(Matthew 25:40)

Most of us look for friendships among people from the same social and economic strata and with whom we share common interests. We usually don't waste time trying to develop relationships with people who are different from us. However, when we do go beyond the steps of how most acquaintances develop, we're sometimes surprised to discover true friendship.

When my older brother was a student at A&M University, he wrote us that he was bringing home a new Aggie friend. I assumed his friend would be like my brother, and I clearly remember my astonishment when they walked up the sidewalk. My anglo brother, who was five feet nine inches tall, was with a Chinese young man who was probably six feet three inches tall. As we laughed and enjoyed that weekend together, I realized that while there were significant dissimilarities between my brother and his college comrade, they had nevertheless developed a true friendship.

One Sunday during the height of the "hippie culture" on Peachtree Street in Atlanta, Georgia, a young couple from that area walked three miles to our church for morning worship. They didn't have a car, but they had a television and had heard the regular telecasts of our Sunday services. Feeling a sense of pride, I thought they had come to hear my husband's great sermons, but they actually came to hear the talented violinist who played each Sunday morning.

Lisa and David soon joined our church, and Lisa came into my Sunday School class of typical twenty-year-old Atlanta women. Unlike the other members of my class, Lisa had long straight hair, small round glasses, and wore an ankle-length print dress. I could feel the tension and prayed that in spite of the obvious differences, she would be accepted into this traditional group. I will always be grateful for the warm reception the other young women gave her, and it wasn't long before deep friendships were made, and Lisa and David and their little boy were being blessed and blessing us with their presence.

On other occasions, furloughing missionaries with their children would come to Atlanta from an international location to live in our church's missionary house. If their children were teenagers, they could speak several languages, had traveled to many places on the globe, and sometimes had been in the center of exciting world events. But the thing that impressed the teenagers in our church was that these missionary children had never driven a car! That was unbelievable to the kids who had lived in the United States all of their lives. But again, in spite of the differences, friendships were soon made and the lives of both "home-bodies" and "new-comers" were enriched.

People usually don't seek friendships among those who are unlike them. Living as we do in a scientific and technological culture with its proven laboratory procedures and clear-cut mathematical formulas makes us more comfortable with things that are predictable and familiar. We're skittish about involvement with unpredictables that can't be readily calculated – like making friends with people who are different.

But we forget that joy and satisfaction aren't always found in the comfort zones of conventional formulas. They sometimes appear in the surprising, unexpected serendipities of life. Friendship is more closely akin to the unpredictable swirls, spirals, and rhythms of art and music than it is to the straight-line routines of math and science. So we should be more open to the possibility of being "surprised by joy" when we reach out to people who are different.

It's especially challenging to make friends among people who are not only different but unlovely and unappealing. Sometimes circumstances create bitterness and hostility in persons that discourage any attempt to be friends with them. So most of us give up, regarding such unbearable personalities as "throw away scraps." They forget that "scraps" can be nurtured like compost into good rich soil. With a little patience, one might discover in these difficult people an opportunity for new and unexpected companionship.

Our efforts at developing friendships can be either intentional or unintentional. If we see someone in need and deliberately make plans to be a friend and meet their need – that's intentional friend-making. Unintentional friend-making on the other hand, is a matter of a day-by-day lifestyle, a friendly outlook that habitually sees others as important. There's a proverb that says, "She who would have friends must show herself friendly."

Befriending a person from another culture or reaching out to an unlikely, unlovable antagonist not only adds interest and enrichment to our lives, but it can also contribute to a more peaceful world as bridges are built and trust is developed. Let's let our compass lead us to be both intentional and unintentional friends

ENDURING FRIENDSHIPS

"A friend loves at all times..."
(Proverbs 17:17)

When I was a freshman at Baylor University, like all entering students (of that era), I wore the traditional freshman cap – a green and gold beanie which upper classmen called a "slime cap." A new friend, Doug Dillard, printed my name and the year of my class in bold letters above the bill.

Both my husband and I are Baylor graduates, and we could hardly wait for our first child to be big enough to wear a miniature version of the Baylor "slime cap." This small version had printed on it "Class of 19?" In a pathetic example of parental brain washing, he was wearing his Baylor slime cap when he was only two years old!

This little boy grew up, and he did become a Baylor graduate. He married and had a little boy of his own, and when they were visiting us one time I ran up to the attic and found that same little Baylor "slime cap" his daddy had worn. I put it on our grandson's head thinking, "How cute! This family tradition would extend to a third generation." But our son shook his head and quickly exclaimed," Mom, he can't wear that! It says 19? If Harrison graduates from Baylor it will be 2008!"

Things change. Familiar possessions become unusable. The electric typewriter has become the word processor. Louis L'amour paperbacks are no longer read while driving west because we have audio tapes and CDs to listen to. We don't see those little scraps of paper and the tiny golf pencils at library counters anymore because computers have taken over the card file. We could list countless other changes that have made products unusable.

But in the turbulence of all this swirling change, real friendships never become outdated or unusable. A friend is a person well known, respected, and loved. A friend is forgiving, shares her feelings when bad things happen and when good things happen. She is loyal, and like good medicine, she reduces the pain and lifts you up. Cicero said "friendship throws a greater luster on prosperity, while it lightens adversity by sharing in its griefs and anxieties."

The new friend, Doug Dillard, who printed my name and class year on my Baylor slime cap, has remained a friend for over fifty years. Recently when his wife died, we shared in his grief. And then some time later, when he remarried, we also joined in his joy.

A psychological study of women has concluded that a woman's sense of self-worth is grounded in her ability to make and maintain friendships. That's one reason women use conversation to initiate, grow, and understand friendships. That's why invitations to "come for coffee" or "come for tea" become moments of reaching out to stimulate friendships. Friendships color every aspect of a woman's life. Sometimes, these friendships result from a common interest or hobbies shared between two persons. These common interests become a bridge between race and culture and contribute to a more peaceful and equal world.

Enormous changes occur every day, but the importance of enduring friendships will never change.

POEMS OF FRIENDSHIPS
Written by Charis Smith

If life were true to the laws of math
And followed rules of parallelism,
Our lines would have been drawn straight and equidistant
Never becoming any closer.

Einstein proved, though, that straight lines
Do bend as they reach out into space.
So you, who write numbers to order your way,
Taught your hand and heart to use words to better define
your shape.

I, who truly believe that "a word fitly spoken
Is like apples of gold in frames of silver",
Heard with my listening ear the divisions and subdivisions
Of Bach's mathematical beat.

I opened my seeing eye to universal patterns
Created by formulae.
My straight lines became curves, swirls and spirals,
That rose, fell, touched and intersected.

Lord, make me a compost person.
Put me in an out of the way place,
Unconcerned about sweet smells of sacrifice or noble
recognition.

Let me be a receptacle for scraps:
To those who are less than whole;
Surface parings, bruised flesh, and hard inner cores.
Help me be one who turns and mixes,

So time and warmth result in a creation,
Of soil from which new life flourishes.
(CHARIS SMITH, A RETIRED TEACHER AND
LIBRARIAN, IS A FRIEND OF THE AUTHOR AND A
MEMBER OF SOUTH MAIN BAPTIST CHURCH IN
HOUSTON, TEXAS.)

A COMPASS FOR ACTION

MAY WE USE YOUR BOXES?

"We are therefore Christ's ambassadors."
(2 Corinthians 5:20)

It was a hot July day, and we had just moved into the president's home on the campus of Southwestern seminary. We had put many of our empty moving boxes at the curb behind our house. Moving again was certainly not in my thoughts, and I had no desire to keep any of those commercial moving boxes in the attic! They were useless to me.

Our back doorbell rang early the next morning, and I went to answer it. I was greeted by an attractive young woman who quickly explained that she and her husband were seminary students and lived across the street from us in a little white house. As she spoke, she gestured toward the house. Then she excitedly proclaimed that her husband had just graduated in the July commencement, and they had been called to a church in another state. "Could we possibly use your moving boxes?" she asked.

"Yes, yes," I answered, "Of course. I'll help you take them across to your house." As we transported empty boxes across the street, my new friend kept up a steady conversation about their joy and anticipation in moving to their first church.

I couldn't help but remember our first churches and the moves we encountered. The first one was 80 miles from Fort Worth, and we had traveled there every week-end for four years, staying in the small, but very adequate and clean two-room parsonage next door to the church. Later, when we moved to the six-room parsonage in Clifton, Texas to "live on the field," it also was an exciting time. I experienced in a second-hand way the joy my new friend was describing.

Because of my boxes, I was having a part in her new life and ministry. What I had discarded that had been of no use to me was being used in a new beginning. That day God gave me the encouraging insight that my husband and I and this graduating seminary couple were serving in the same calling - ambassadors for Christ wherever we might be sent.

I DIDN'T EVEN MAKE THE BED

"Offer hospitality to one another without
grumbling."
(1 Peter 4:9)

My first entertaining experience in our home was an OPEN HOUSE and I wasn't even there. Russell and I had been married three weeks. My husband was a seminary student and the new pastor of the Antelope Baptist Church in a community about 80 miles north of Fort Worth, Texas. On Friday afternoon we had driven to Antelope to spend the weekend in the little two-room parsonage next door to the church building. We were so grateful that volunteers from the membership had worked hard to redecorate and refurnish our small but convenient week-end home.

On this first Sunday we had awakened early and were looking over the Sunday school lesson and the sermon for the day. Knowing that Sunday school began at 9:30, we felt we had plenty of time to dress and walk over to the church. Having both been reared in cities, Russell and I didn't know that people in rural communities come very early to church in order to visit with their neighbors.

When we saw the pick up trucks driving into the church parking area we sprang into action. Hurriedly, we finished dressing, left the unmade bed with the brand new red chenille bedspread on the floor, clothes on chairs, new quilts spilling out of the chest and dirty breakfast dishes in the sink, and walked quickly next door to the church. Our only thought was to get there in time to meet our new church members.

After worship, I walked toward the front door of the church where Russell was shaking hands with the congregation, and I had the fright of my life! Upon leaving the church every one of the 64 members had walked across the hard packed dirt of west Texas into the side door of the parsonage, were passing through the two rooms, and exiting by the front door! I was mortified. All I could think of was the new bedspread on the floor in the corner of the bedroom, the unmade bed and the dirty dishes in the sink. I could just hear the words of the members saying, "Sweet little bride. She doesn't even know how to make the bed"

I quickly ran and hid behind the piano. After Russell shook hands with the last person, he came to me and with alarm on his face asked me what I was doing? I took him to the church window and pointed to our house! We both waited in the church until every pickup truck had left.

That evening two unmarried sisters, Miss. Myrtle and Miss Eva, came up to me after the service and said, "We want to apologize for our actions this morning. Everyone was so excited about the redecorating of the parsonage that we just walked in, and it's not our house. It's yours and we're sorry."

Mustering up all of my courage and a friendly smile, I could only mumble with a very red face, "Oh, that's all right. Come back anytime."

Needless to say since that time I've tried to be better prepared for guests.

Having guests in your home can be a rich experience for both you and your guests. In this day when there is so much moving from place to place, from city to city and even state-to-state, I can't think of anything more needed than the spirit of hospitality. Many people are lonely and feel unaccepted. Having people in your home strengthens relationships, erases misunderstandings, and above all communicates God's love. Hospitality is also encouraged in scripture. Romans 12:13 says *"Contributing to the needs of the saints, practicing hospitality."*

There is no better place in this inhospitable world than a shared Christian home. There is no greater complement you can give someone than to invite them into your home for refreshments.

In knowing and esteeming others with gracious hospitality we show them an example that might ignite the gift of service in them.

IT'S ABOUT TIME!

There is a time for everything, and a season for
every activity under heaven.
(Ecclesiastes 3:1)

In today's pressure cooker world, we're controlled by time. It makes demands on all of us. It's time "to go," "to work," "to talk." Most of us think we don't have enough time in a day to do all we want to do.

Not many of us would identify with the woman who wrote to Dear Abby some years ago in the newspaper. Her letter said that by 8:30 every morning she had completed all household responsibilities and was totally bored with women who lamented over all the work they had to do! We would identify more readily with the woman who said, "Anybody whose work is done is either numb or very dumb."

Time is a flexible concept that we each experience differently. That's why Shakespeare said, "For some people time ambles; for others it trots or gallops, and for some it stands still." To a child in a car, driving to the beach on a family vacation, an hour can seem like eternity. All of us have heard a child in the car say, "Are we there, yet?"

For adults, being on a diet or waiting for a doctor's diagnosis can seem a very long time, and yet, time can seem very short when you're enjoying a beautiful sunset, or a visit from a long time friend whom you haven't seen in many years, or when you put a stack of old pictures in a scrapbook and you see how your children have changed. We agree with Shakespeare when he said, "Time gallops"

All of us have the same 24 hours each day, but some people are able to get more done in a day than others. When a child was asked, "What's the difference between moms and dads," she answered, "Moms work at work, and at home, but dads just work at work." The same child was asked what her mom did in her spare time and she answered, "My mom doesn't do spare time." That's why the phrase "working mother" is redundant.

Each day is a gift from God for which we are to rejoice and be glad, but we are also responsible for using each day wisely. That isn't easy in our hectic, fast-paced society, but here are some suggestions.

(1) <u>Learn how to prioritize the 24 hours God gives us each day</u>. A guide for the Christian woman is found in Matthew 6:33 *"Seek ye first His kingdom and His righteousness (God's) and all these things will be given to you as well."* Because there are so many opportunities today, the Christian woman is usually not faced with choosing between good and bad, but between what is good and what is best. So we are forced to set priorities ranking what is urgent and what can wait until tomorrow.

In *Gone with the Wind,* when Scarlett said, "I'll think about that tomorrow," most people accused her of procrastination. But the fact is there really are some things that can wait until tomorrow. Some tasks are daily and regular. Making a list of goals for a week and a list of tasks for each day may help us give priority to our time.

(2) <u>Remember that people are more important than time schedules</u>. Some women are so geared to achieving their lists that they overlook people. Don't forget, the Bible says, *"Whatever you did for one of the least of these brothers of mine, you did for me."*

(3) <u>Don't dwell on past mistakes</u>. Guilt is a big energy drainer. Consider each new day as a "beginning again" time. Be encouraged by the words of the apostle, "Forgetting what is behind, I press on toward the goal for which God has called me."

(4) <u>Keep in mind that each segment of time has its special privileges and responsibilities</u>. The Bible says there

is a time for everything under the sun. That includes child-bearing, parenting, schooling, caring for aging parents, and a catalogue of similar responsibilities. Experiences that might otherwise defeat us can become rewarding occasions for learning if we realize that God is with us during these periods.

(5) <u>Balance your left and right brain functions</u>. The left side of the brain is for rules, priorities, and schedules while the right brain is the fun side and is creative and artistic. It's not easy for a left brain person to take time for fun and creativity, and it's even harder for a light-hearted right brain person to settle down and give attention to schedules and obligations. But remember, a genius has been defined as an ordinary person who has learned to balance her brain. Take courage from the fact that as you struggle today to balance your time and your brain, you can be extraordinary. You can be a genius.

Let's be grateful for the days God gives us. Prioritize your tasks, put people first, forget past mistakes, realize each day has its special purpose, and balance your brain. It's about time you became a genius!

MY GOODNESS! THE CABOOSE IS GREEN!

"I, the Lord, do not change."
(Malachi 3:6)

I was driving through Ft. Worth with my granddaughter when we came to a railroad crossing. The barricades were slowly coming down, indicating that a train was approaching. As we sat there in our car watching the train roll past, I tried to interest Elizabeth in counting the cars with me. It was a long train and soon she became bored. I reminded her about the little red caboose, the last car that's always at the end of the train, and we started singing the little song, "Little Red Caboose, Chug, Chug, and Chug." As the train came to an end, the last car - the caboose - whizzed past us.

"Look, Nana," cried Elizabeth, "It's not red; it's GREEN!" Sure enough, the traditional red caboose had been changed to green.

How do you react to change? Is it a friend or an enemy? Change is inevitable, and it's everywhere. There can be no life without change.

I used to think that my mother's generation saw the most change. I remember her telling me that she heard about the end of World War I from a newsboy hollering "Extra, Extra, read all about it" as she stood on a Houston street corner waiting for the street car to take her to her first teaching position.

But the overwhelming changes of these last years have set our heads spinning. Everything that was nailed or glued down is coming loose. The demise of the Soviet Union, the fall of the Berlin wall, the emerging of new countries such as Slovakia and Bosnia, international terrorism, the changing role of women, and technological innovations that have brought us the cell phone, E-mail, and on-line shopping, all have affected us. But the changes which seem to affect us most are the aging of our parents and their care; rising health and college tuition costs; the safety of our children in schools or in our backyards, the breakdown of the family by divorce, and the complexity of the extended family. Even the tried, old recipes of past generations can no longer be used because our stores don't carry the same ingredients.

But change can be beneficial. Where would we be today if air-conditioning were not a given in our lives? Antibiotics and the marvelous advances in medical surgery have given us longer and healthier lives. Air travel makes tourism and seeing loved ones much easier. We could name many changes which have made life better for us.

The younger generation is discovering innovative new ways to improve age-old tasks, making life more enjoyable. I heard Shirley Dobson tell of a young mother of two children who one day found her four-year-old daughter playing with the 9 months old baby brother in another room of the house. Fearing that the four-year-old might try to carry the younger child and even drop him, the mother quickly admonished her daughter. "You must not carry your little brother." But the four-year-old daughter quickly responded, "Oh, Mother, I don't carry him, I just *ROLL* him!"

We can be assured that in this next millennium the changes will come even more rapidly. A lot of things that used to be carried are going to be rolled!

We are overwhelmed by the unpredictable turbulence that surprises us every day and more will come. But we can be assured that Jesus Christ will never change. His love will always be limitless and his sufficiency all-encompassing. Circumstances may change, friends may change, our physical bodies will change; but the character and promises of God will never change.

NOT UNTIL YOU SAY THANK YOU

"It is good to give thanks to the Lord..."
(Psalm 92:1)

A young family had just had their second child, a little boy. Many friends were coming by their house with a gift for the new baby but also with a gift for his four-year-old sister. As the daddy and the little girl met the friends at the door, the visitors would first give their gift to the sister of the newborn. She would grab it and run off to her room to open the surprise. Her daddy would admonish her to say "thank you," but she never did.

Exasperated the father began taking the child's gift himself and not letting her have it until she said "thank you" to the giver. However, this didn't work too well because the little sister pouted and ran to her room without saying thank you and without the gift. Finally one day she reluctantly began responding to the visitors with a thank you and the father gave her the gifts.

In this world where gratitude is so often overlooked, I was glad to see a parent trying to teach thankfulness to his daughter, even at a young age. True, her "thank you" began as a rote exercise and as a necessary condition for getting the present, but the principle of thankfulness was being taught.

There was a man in our church who had become very successful in his work, even though he grew up with very few privileges as a child and had dropped out of school in the fourth grade. At Thanksgiving he gave a frozen turkey to every one on the church staff. One day he told me that most of the staff never thanked him for the turkey. They acted like they just expected it. I remembered that line from Shakespeare, "How sharper than a serpent's tooth it is to have a thankless child," and the wise observation of Henry

Ward Beecher, "A proud man is seldom a grateful man, but he never thinks he gets as much as he deserves."

Sybil Armes wrote that an attitude of thankfulness is the candle of the human spirit; it warms the heart and illumines the countenance. We all like to hear expressions of thankfulness from our children and others. How much more does the heart of God rejoice when we say thank you to Him for all His benefits to us. Let us be ones who thank Him.

OH, THOSE WORDS

*"He who guards his mouth and his tongue, keeps
himself from calamity."*
(Proverbs 21:23)

One morning, not long ago our daughter welcomed a new member of her church. The two soon became good friends. One day as they were chatting about their parents, their childhood homes, and other things, the friend said to our daughter, "Oh, are you a Dilday? Is Betty Dilday your mother?"

Ellen, thinking the friend would say something good about her mother, smiled and said, "Yes, she is."

Then the friend went on to say, (laughingly, I hope) "Well, she once told me I shouldn't wear a halter dress to church."

Needless to say, I was embarrassed when my daughter told me of this incident. In all of the years of teaching the Bible, visiting the unchurched, encouraging the sick, and trying to be "salt in the earth," the only thing this girlfriend could remember were these critical words I'd said!

Negative words. Judgmental words. How often do we say things that do nothing to build up a person? How many times do we chatter about trivia when we could be telling good news?

My mother-in-law many years ago told me that old people talk too much. They go on and on talking, probably because of loneliness. But she always admonished me that as she grew older, it was my duty to notice if she talked too much and tell her to stop. (Of course, I never did)

But it isn't just older people who talk too much and say useless or hurtful things. All of are guilty sometimes. Maybe that's why the Bible has a lot to say about the tongue. It's a small muscle of the body but oh, how those words the tongue speaks can come back to make you ashamed.

Lord, help me to speak words of encouragement, edification, and comfort. *"Reckless words pierce like a sword, but the tongue of the wise brings healing."*
Proverbs 12:18

QUESTIONS

*"I have seen and I testify that this is
the Son of God.*
(John 1:34)

I like people. I'm curious about new friends, and so I ask questions. My children have teased me for years that when meeting new people, I always ask two questions immediately: "Where did you grow up?" and "Where do you go to church?"

I'm always looking for a "handle" to help me remember a new acquaintance, some common ground to foster a friendship. Most of those I meet answer my questions gladly, giving me the name of their hometown and their church membership. From those answers I can usually find some mutual friends or common interest, and a friendship begins.

I was talking with two friends the other day, and one of them shared an unfortunate experience. When she asked a new acquaintance where she went to church, the person answered, "It's none of your business." I was as shocked. We all agreed that sometimes our words are misunderstood. We unknowingly offend.

We also agreed there might be a better way of sharing our faith and the joy of our church life than asking pointblank, "Where do you go to church?" It might be better to begin talking about events in our own church - the fun, the caring fellowship, the support we enjoy because we belong to a church family. The new friend will probably ask, "Where do you go to church?" Then the door is open to find out more about her spiritual experience and church relationship.

So I'm trying hard to change and give up my two favorite questions, "Where did you grow up?" and "Where do you go to church?" It'll be hard, but maybe in the long run I'll learn more about a new acquaintance using a less threatening, indirect approach than my old way!

WE'LL BE HAPPY THERE

"But godliness with contentment is great gain."
(1Timothy 6:6)

I was teaching the Bible passage about Abraham's call from God to leave his home in Ur and move with his family to an unknown and unfamiliar area. Since I teach a large class of women, I focused for a short time on how Sara must have felt about moving. I asked my class about their moving experiences. How many times had they moved? What had been the problems? How had they felt?

Some had moved five or six times but one class member, Cissy, whose husband had become an admiral in the United States Navy, had moved 34 times in 36 years. We all gasped, but she was quick to assure us that sometimes it was just to larger quarters on the same base, maybe just across the street from her present home. It may not have entailed leaving a familiar place or old friends, but it did mean "packing up" and restructuring her home life.

Adeanya and Joe Hunt were friends of ours for many years. Joe worked for Southwestern Bell Telephone Company, and in 24 years they had moved 15 times. Adeanya found a clever way to help her family quickly feel "at home" in their new surroundings. She made a pattern in brown paper of the picture arrangement over her living room sofa. As soon as the movers had placed the sofa in the new house, Adeanya whipped out her pattern, taped it to the wall above the sofa, marked where the nails would be, and had the familiar picture arrangement in place in the blink of an eye!

But this was not the only thing they did in order to feel "at home" quickly in the new location. Within three weeks they had joined the nearest Baptist church, were in Sunday School, and had joined the choir!

Moving from one place to another many times is not an easy experience for us women. Whether you're a minister's wife, a military wife, or the wife of a business executive, there is a feeling of anxiety about what's ahead. Holding on to the comfortable familiarity of what "has been" and dreading the change is a sure way of making life in the new location miserable.

Each semester as new students arrived on the campus of Southwestern seminary, I knew that some would adjust quickly to the flat Texas terrain, the hot summers, and student housing. I knew it would take others longer than it should to appreciate the gorgeous Texas sunsets that cover the whole horizon because they would still be pining for the Florida seashore, the Mississippi trees, the Colorado Rockies, or the Georgia dogwood of their former homes.

Here are some suggestions that may be helpful in adjusting and being happy in a new location. (1) Go to a new place with the idea of putting down roots. Don't think of a move as a temporary stop on the way to another place. (2) Keep your mind open to find good things about the new area. I had lived in Texas all my life, so when we moved to Georgia I quickly read Eugenia Price's books about Georgia – *The Lighthouse, Beloved Invader,* and *New Moon Rising.* While in the state I was delighted to read the trilogies she continued to write about the area. (3) See a move as an opportunity to change bad habits. It may be easier to become more disciplined in a place where no one knows you. (4) If the services you've rendered in certain areas of your church or school are not needed in your new situation, find other places of service. (5) Accept the fact that some things are done differently in certain parts of the country and try to adjust and understand these ways of doing things rather than resenting them.

And finally, read Philippians 4:11 (over and over if need be,) *"For I have learned to be content in whatever circumstances I am."* If your spiritual compass points in God's direction, then you'll find happiness there.

WHAT CAN *I* DO?

"Each one should use whatever gift he has
received to serve others."
(1 Peter 4:10)

Janice was the young wife of a youth minister in a Baptist church. She was attractive and uninhibited, and sometimes her blunt comments raised the eyebrows of the older women in the congregation. One day she was sharing with me the frustration she felt in trying to find her special place to serve in the church. She didn't feel comfortable doing some of the tasks typically expected of a youth minister's wife, such as teaching in Sunday School.

I'm not sure my advice was very helpful that day, but Janice was a very creative person, and she found a unique ministry that particularly impressed our two daughters. The next Christmas, she came by our house and presented the pastor's family with a beautifully decorated Christmas gingerbread house. It could have made the cover of "Good Housekeeping!" Of course, my two daughters had a mother who couldn't create a work of art like that culinary masterpiece, if she had worked for weeks! They thought Janice was the most wonderful and talented minister's wife they had ever seen.

Some years later we had moved to Ft. Worth, Texas where Russell had become president of Southwestern Baptist Theological Seminary, and we were celebrating our first Christmas season in the president's home. Our daughters were home from college and since their father was no longer a pastor, they were missing the love and (the gifts) that a congregation always gave to their preacher's family – that is, until one day shortly before December 25. On that day, Janice, whose youth minister husband had become the Minister of Education at First Baptist Church, Denton, Texas, walked up to the door of our home on campus with – you guessed it - another beautiful, "Good Housekeeping" gingerbread house – this time in the shape of a church!

I often think of Janice when reluctant people ask, "What can *I* do?" By looking at her gifts, showing concern for others, and putting her ability into action, Janice shared a unique ministry that was totally hers and that will never be forgotten. She will be forever appreciated.

WHAT IS THAT IN YOUR HAND?

*"Then the Lord said to him (Moses), 'What is that
in your hand?'"*
(Exodus 4:2)

I was in the beautiful home of a friend recently and saw on the wall in her bedroom two lovely bridal portraits of her daughters. Nearby was a photograph of another bride, which my friend laughingly identified as her own bridal picture. I asked if either of her girls had worn her beautiful white dress and she responded they had not. After a moment of hesitation, she explained, "My wedding dress is actually in Africa now."

When she saw my quizzical expression, she explained that a long-time missionary friend had asked at a luncheon one day if anyone had a wedding dress that young Christian women in her African community could wear when they had pictures made of their wedding day. They wanted to remember the event dressed in a beautiful white gown. Remembering her own wedding dress safely boxed up under her bed, she responded to the request, and gave it to her missionary friend for Christian brides to wear when their pictures were made.

As an afterthought my friend said, "I've received pictures of the African women wearing my dress, and I guess I should frame them and arrange them around my portrait." Her "loss" of not seeing her daughter or granddaughter in her wedding dress was "gained" by seeing the joy on the smiling faces of the young African women dressed in white on their wedding day. Of course, her gift brought enormous joy to her own heart as well.

Moses felt totally inadequate when God called him to free the people of Israel from Pharaoh, so God asked him, "What is that in your hand?" All Moses had was an ordinary staff, but God used it to work miracles and free the people. (Exodus 4:2) What do you have in your hand?

Many of us have unused possessions boxed up in our attics or under our beds that with a little creative imagination could bring joy not only to needy recipients, but also to us, the givers. What do you have in your hand? Many of us have abundant talent and abilities in our hands. Some are expert cooks, and they can prepare a wonderful meal. Friends can be invited to your home for an evening dinner or these delicacies could be taken to a new neighbor on your street, to a sick friend, or to a lonely, elderly person who has lost interest in cooking for herself. What do you have in your hand?

Others have the artistic ability to crochet, embroider, or make beautiful needlepoint gifts. Since handwork is not one of my talents, I'm always thrilled to receive gifts like those.

What do you have in your hand? Moses had an ordinary walking stick. You might be surprised how God can use your "ordinary" skills and possessions to do wonderful things for Him and for others. *"Whatever your hand finds to do, do it with your might."* (Eccl. 9:10)

WITNESSING

*"I planted the seed, Apollos watered it, but God
made it grow. So neither he who plants nor the one
who waters is anything...."*
(1 Corinthians. 3:6, 7)

The irate preacher rushed up to me and angrily spouted
out the words, "How many people have you won to the Lord
this week?" I was astounded at his spirit and found myself
momentarily speechless. Later, I remembered my experience
in Atlanta when I became acquainted with a young woman,
named Linda who worked at a local bank. She was married
and had several small children, but she and her family didn't
attend church. I invited her to attend the Sunday school class
I was teaching, and when she accepted my invitation, I had
frequent opportunities to speak to her about becoming a
Christian.

One Sunday she made a public profession of faith in
Christ in our church, and needless to say, I felt a little self-
righteous. "Look what I've done," I thought, "I've led her to
Jesus Christ!" But during the next week, as she and I were
talking about her new experience in Christ, she told me, "I'm
so grateful for Bruce, my colleague at the bank, because he
helped me so much in becoming a Christian."

I knew Bruce. He was a deacon in our church. All the
sudden my self-righteous bubble burst! I thought I had been
the one who won her to Christ. Didn't my witness have any
affect?

Recently, I heard a young Chinese woman give her
testimony about how she came to accept Christ as her
savior. Lucy was studying microbiology and Chemistry in a
Shanghai University where her father was a professor. The
university encouraged Baptist Women from the United States
to come for short periods of time to teach English, and in

1994, several women from my church in Texas accepted the invitation and went to Shanghai. Lucy joined their English class where they used the Bible as one of the text books.

Lucy had always thought of the Bible as a book of fairy tales, especially the book of Genesis which she believed conflicted with her scientific evolution studies. She felt it would be impossible to be a scientist and a Christian at the same time. She said "her head and heart "didn't seem to go together.

After leaving China, these women kept in touch with Lucy, sending her academic and Christian periodicals, and making international phone calls. They encouraged her in her studies and told her they were praying for her.

Several years later when the women returned to China, they sought out Lucy and continued their friendship. It was during one of these visits, on May 1, 1998 (she was emphatic as to the date), Lucy became a Christian.

Since then, Lucy has witnessed to her parents who have become Christians. She came to America, earned two Masters Degrees, and joined a group called "International Christian Fellowship" that witnesses to international students in Dallas universities. From this rich background, she teaches other international Christians how they can share their faith.

Winning people to Christ is not cutting a notch on your belt when you've made a conquest, because usually a person's decision to accept Christ is the result of the cumulative influence of several persons. Everyone's witness is effective. Paul wrote that the one who plants and the one who waters are both God's fellow workers who share in telling the good news of Christ.

Let's be humble and grateful that we have the privilege of being partners with other witnesses in leading unbelievers to the life-changing experience of knowing Jesus Christ as their Lord and Savior.

YOU NEED A HUG

*"Therefore, as we have opportunity, let us
do good to all people..."*
(Galatians 6:10)

I get some of my philosophy of life from the comic strips. *Kathy, Peanuts,* and *Family Circus* have provided me with some valuable insights. Recently, I was reminded in *Family Circus* the value of a "hug." According to the comic strip, a hug relieves tension, helps self-esteem, and generates good will. It doesn't cost anything; it doesn't require any batteries; it's non-taxable, and it's extremely personal. Most of all it is recommended for ages one to a hundred.

The importance of these words came to life for me some time ago when I picked up my grandson at his preschool. We were walking down the hall toward the door to the parking lot, when we saw the principal of the school. She was walking slowly and had a worried and fretful look on her face. But her countenance brightened somewhat when she saw us. We stopped to talk and soon she began to tell me of the awful events that had occurred during that day and some of the problems she was still facing. The electricity had been going on and off, a sick child had been diagnosed with chicken pox by the school nurse, no one had volunteered to chair the school's field day, and there were other challenges multiplying even as we talked.

Andrew, then four years old, tugged on my slacks and said, "Nana, I think Mrs. Smith needs a hug." Laughing, Mrs. Smith picked up Andrew and said, "You're right, Andrew, I sure do," and he squeezed her tight.

Hugs are a perfect gift. They're non-polluting and fully returnable.

But, we're often too busy to notice people or hear about the frustrations they face in their daily lives.

After our visit with Mrs. Smith, the principal, Andrew and I went on to our car. When we looked back, Mrs. Smith seemed to hold her shoulders straighter, and walk a little more briskly. Somehow I felt her hug from Andrew had added a needed spark to help her face and accomplish the jobs she needed to do.

A popular slogan on car bumpers read, "Have you hugged your child today?" Obviously, encouragement and showing love and concern are needed by all of us, whether we are young or older. Let's look for those moments when we can be that spark of encouragement – even if it's as simple as a hug.

Printed in the United States
129636LV00002B/1-150/P

9 781606 479483